The Face in the Window

Out, Standing in My Field

The Face in the Window
A Guide to Professional Dog Walking

2ND EDITION INCLUDES:

Out, Standing in My Field
A Guide to Home Boarding

Dianne Eibner

JOG-A-DOG BOOKS
Toronto 2000

First Published 1999
Revised 2006
Copyright © 1999, 2006 by Dianne Eibner

Printed in Canada by Webcom Limited

First Edition, The Face In The Window - Edited by:
Jean Cockburn Editing Services
Second Edition, edited by Carolyn Russell
Photographs by Christina Winchur, Lisa M. Jones and Dianne Eibner
Cover Illustration copyright © 2006 by Catherine Gillespie
Typesetting and Design by Nancy Reid

Library and Archives Canada Cataloguing in Publication

Eibner, Dianne, 1971-
The face in the window: a guide to professional dogwalking/Dianne
Eibner. -- 2nd ed., includes: Out, standing in my field: a guide to home boarding

ISBN 0-9687008-2-9

1. Dog walking.   2. New business enterprises
I. Title.   II. Title: Out, standing in my field.

SF427.46.E35 2006   636.7'0887   C2005-906412-9

JOG-A-DOG BOOKS
157 Goose Lake Rd. RR#3
Woodville, Ont. K0M 2T0

Email: jogadog@sympatico.ca
Website: www.jogadog.ca

The Face in the Window was nominated, "Best Short Book"
by the Dog Writer's Assoc. of America, 2000.

Contents

PART II: **Out, Standing in My Field**
A Guide to Home Boarding

Preface

The title *The Face in the Window*, refers to the many furry faces I have seen peering out the windows of their homes as I drive up to relieve them of their monotony. They wait for me. Sometimes I believe that they are checking the clock for the time. That is, only if I happen to be a few minutes late. And they know it. I've been told that the dogs get all excited when they hear a car drive slowly by their house. Dogs have internal clocks and they relate to scheduling. Fergus, a Golden Retriever, sits at the door and looks out. When a car goes by that doesn't pull up into his driveway, he takes a great big breath and then...sigh... "Don't worry Fergus, I'm on my way!" Shakes, a German Shepherd, would pace back and forth the minute that twelve noon passed. He'd run from the front door to the back door then back again looking out the window for me. By five after twelve he would start to get vocal and whine. "Where is she? Where is she?" I learned these things about the dogs when the owners happened to be home that day. I guess the owners learned about their dogs too, because they'd tell me," I've never seen him act this way before."

This is not a book about how to train dogs. This is a book about professional dog walking and in this second edition, I have included *Out, Standing in My Field - A Guide to Home Boarding*. These are my own personal experiences and what has worked for me. This book, I hope, will be used as a guide for those who have started or are thinking of starting a dogwalking or pet care company. I would like this book to give you some insight into the kind of situations and predicaments that might occur in the midst of your outings. Perhaps this book will help you decide if this is the right realm of employment for you. Whether dog walking appeals to you as a sole proprietorship or employment for a larger company, this book should help you decide what suits your lifestyle and make the right decision for everyone's sake.

It was in 1990 when I was just out of high school and trying to find a job, when I saw an ad in a local paper: "Responsible boy, girl or adult to take two large (but friendly) sheepdogs for a walk in the late afternoon Monday to Friday." I met the sheepdogs on a Friday and started on Monday. In 1992, I stopped trying to maintain "dead-end" part-time jobs and started focusing on the dog walking. By the year 2000, I moved my business to the country and focused on boarding dogs. Since then...

"It was the best thing I could've done for myself. The best part about running your own business of pet care isn't about being your own boss it's about being able to work with animals. The stories in this book are all true accounts and they are but a few of the incidents that I have experienced. I would like anyone who thinks they want to do this to know they have to put their heart and soul into it."

Acknowledgements

Thank you to Boston "Cream Puff" for being my face in the window.

A special thank you to Lisa M. Jones for helping me put it all together. Please visit her web site at: www.lmjmusic.com

I would like to dedicate this book to everyone that believed in and appreciated me. I would like to thank them for their support, encouragement, enlightenment and inspiration over the past 10 years, without whom this book would not have been possible. Incidentally, 90% of them have four legs.

I would also like to thank all the uneducated people whom I have had the opportunity to meet and experience.

Most importantly, I want to acknowledge and say thank you to my clients for trusting and supporting me. Lastly, I would like to dedicate this book to my very first clients, the sheepdogs, Cindy and Snow.

PART ONE

The Face in the Window
A Guide to Professional Dog Walking

Chapter 1

Characteristics of Dogs in a Group

It never fails. The different personalities and characteristics of dogs in a group can be compared with kids in a classroom. There's always the class clown, the troublemaker, the jock, the shy one, the accident prone one, and the teacher's pet.

When you get three, four, five or six dogs together, you can see a pack mentality and the hierarchy among the members of the group forming. One dog is always the "top dog" or "leader" and the others follow suit. Each has their own personality. No matter what type of dogs you have, those personalities seem to repeat when you get a pack together. However, ultimately you are the alpha dog.

Getting to know your dogs' personality is going to help you control them better and have more fun playtime together. When you've got five dogs off leash, you want to make sure you know who's typically going to do what. Then you can prevent anything from happening that you don't want, or at least be prepared when something does happen. For instance, the class clown: You know he's going to do something dopey. Not necessarily dangerous, but he'll usually get everyone else in the group wound up. The troublemaker will get into things you don't want him into. Maybe he's even a bit of a bully. Watch for these types of dogs; you don't want too many in your group because they will need to be supervised more than the others. You don't want them to lead the other dogs with their bad habits.

The jock: Well if this dog could talk he would just keep saying "throw the ball, throw the ball, throw the ball." I've known many jock dogs through the years. Maggie and Timber, both Border Collies, not related and from different owners, have exactly the same characteristics. This breed is so smart, they will make you look like you really know what you're doing. When they were with me I would never have to walk across the field to pick up a ball that another dog had left. I could send Maggie or Timber to go find the ball. It was so neat to watch them discover where the ball was and pick up speed as they zeroed in on it.

The shy one is the timid one of the group. There is usually one dog that takes his or her time to get to know everyone before jumping into a run and play situation. This dog might require a little extra supervision at first and might stand a bit away from the group. Be careful that the shy one doesn't get picked on by the others. Here's an example of a shy dog. When I first met Buddy, a Lab/Retriever mix who was adopted from the Humane Society, he was very uneasy around me. In fact, he tried to bite me a few times. He was very nervous, and didn't like quick movements. At moments during my first visit with him and the client, I would feel pinned and knew if I moved I could get bitten. I avoided eye contact. He wouldn't take biscuits out of my hand so I dropped them on the floor. At least the treats came from me. I was trying to be as non-threatening as possible but this dog was skittish and fearful.

I knew I would have to come over again for another quick visit with the owner and meet Buddy at least once more. We met about three times before I took him out on my own. All three of us went for a walk and even planned for another day to meet up coincidentally in the park. It took about two weeks of walking Buddy to see a change in him and for a trust to develop between us. The first few walks we even had a friend of Buddy's owner wait for me at the house to help get him in the car if needed. Now, I can kiss Buddy on the nose and he'll take biscuits out of my mouth.

One thing I discovered about shy dogs is that some of them don't get into the car as enthusiastically as the others. So one time I decided to jump in the back of the car and then call the dog to come in. It worked that time because I had no other dogs in the car at that point. I have also had to take certain dogs out of the car in order to get another in. But they all learn and get used to hearing terms like "get back."

The accident prone dog is the dog that you end up clocking in the head with a tennis ball or Kong because he ran in front of it at the exact second you threw it. Of course you weren't aiming for him, it's just that this dog has got perfect timing. Or better yet, he's the dog who's paw you stepped on when you were walking backwards and didn't see him hanging around your feet. So when you step on him, you jump up and turn around to see if he's okay and he runs between your legs in all the excitement and then causes you to fall down directly on top of him, again.

Then there is the teacher's pet, the dog that will probably never leave your side. He or she will walk next to you and make you look like a real pro. This type of dog is a big suck. I call this type of dog my shadow. That is what I called Snow, the Sheepdog. Since she passed on, Barclay, a Golden Retriever, now takes on that role. When I first met Barclay, her owner opened the door and the dog ran straight into my arms and has never left my side since. The only thing to watch out for with this type of dog is jealously. This type of dog just might not like

you hugging other dogs too much and may move in between you and the others.

Once you build a clientele, you will notice how your dogs reflect these personalities and you will learn how to handle each one accordingly. Each dog has specific needs. You can learn how to give all the dogs what they need and effectively control a group of dogs off leash.

I did some acting in my earlier days and I picked up a few dialects. I find the dogs are really fascinated when I use an Irish or an English accent when I talk to them. I think they enjoy the high pitches and levels of inflection. Also, don't forget to dance with them every once in a while.

A Collie, named Desi, loved to dance and would join in without missing a beat. Remember that they will have fun if you are having fun.

Howling with your dogs can be fun too, but sometimes I get mixed signals and can't tell if they enjoy it or not. So if they don't seem happy, best not do it. I've found that some dogs howl out of excitement while others it seems like sadness or stress. For example, when I am on my way to the park with a bunch of dogs, out of excitement and anticipation they begin to bark and howl. However, I walked two Spaniels, Max and Joe, who would howl when they heard a distant siren. That doesn't seem like a happy howl. It's hard to tell, but dogs definitely respond to certain sounds and pitches.

Singing to them really excites them too, and when you have their attention that's when you have the opportunity to teach them the kind of behavior you want. I walked a Rhodesian Ridgeback named Makita, and of course the name led me to sing to her 'Chiquita Banana...la...la...la...la...' It didn't take long for her to start responding to Banana more than Makita. It got her attention because she related it to a happy time and she responded to it in a good way. One time I was calling her to come back to me and I was using Makita, but she was not turning around. All of a sudden I called out Banana! She turned on a dime and headed back towards me.

I have my own little temperament test that I try on dogs. I call it the Got Your Nose test. When petting your dog on the head, move your hand slowly down to his muzzle then slide your hand around to your dog's nose. See how long you can cover the nose with your hand. A dog that just sits there and lets you hold onto his nose is a dog with a good temperament towards people. It respects people and knows they are the leaders. Of course, some dogs just have sensitive noses and you should respect that. I have always liked to stretch my limits, so I have kissed their noses, pulled their lips and folded their ears back. Why? I figure, the more they tolerate from me, the more control I have of them overall. I am the Alpha. After a few days we have a real trust and bond and have more fun on our walks. Try sticking your tongue out and wiggling it in front of your dogs and see how they react. Some might just think you're weird — others may see it as an invitation to kiss you.

I walked a German Shepherd named, Houdini. He was an accident prone dog. The poor guy, you name it, it has probably happened to him. As a puppy, he ran into a wall and broke a bone in his front right leg. The fracture affected the way his leg grew and so he has one leg slightly longer than the other, which makes him walk with a bit of a limp now and then. He picked up a virus, which caused him to get warts on the inside of his mouth. He has had "hot spots" or eczema on his neck and body so he had to be shaved everywhere. Houdini has had some bad luck. I once called him the lemon dog because he was like a car that kept breaking down. If there is a piece of glass in the park somewhere, Houdini will find it. But it could be worse. With a name like Houdini, he could've always been disappearing.

There is one characteristic about Houdini that set him apart from all the other dogs and that was his manners. He was such a polite dog. One day I was driving Houdini and a couple other dogs to the park and I heard these gagging sounds. Somebody was getting sick! It's Houdini! I should have quickly pulled over and let him out but it was too late. As I turned my head to look in the back, I saw from the driver's side window a big German Shepherd head and a fountain of doggie puke come flowing out of Houdini's mouth. But it was outside of the car. It wasn't all over me or the others. Houdini had the courtesy to stick his head out the window to throw up. God bless that dog! He was a very smart dog as most German Shepherds are. He was a pleasure to train and picked up new tricks very quickly. On our walks I would teach him to sit periodically. Eventually, I could call out to him from a distance and command him to "sit." If he was running, he would stop in mid stride and "sit." It was a beautiful thing to witness. After a few years in my care, he had to move to England.

LIFE LESSONS LEARNED FROM A DOG:

*If you stare at something long enough,
eventually you'll get what you want.*

Chapter 2

Meeting a New Dog and Client

You can call yourself whatever you want. You can be a Dog Walker, Pet Sitter, Dog Sitter, Professional Walker, Professional Canine Exerciser, Canine Aerobic Stimulator. Whatever the title, we do pretty much the same thing. Even if you're housesitting pets, you'll have to walk some of them eventually. So you might as well be prepared and do it right.

You are not the owner of the dog. You didn't get to raise the dog from a pup. You have to take care and control of this dog you've just met. So you need to know how to read the dog's behaviour quickly and accurately. You need to assess the dog and understand what he is going to need from you. Since you're not the owner or don't know much of the dog's past, asking questions is going to help. However, paying attention to the body language of the dog will give you a lot of the answers.

Before you meet the dog you have to answer the inquiring telephone call or deal with that person asking you questions in the park. There are different types of clients, ones you'll like, and ones that you won't like. When you're just starting out you need clients to help build your reputation so you'll want to take on anyone who calls. Remember that you deserve respect just as much as the caller does.

You might get a call where the person says, "Hi, what do you charge?" Or, "Hi, tell me about your business." Or you'll get a caller that says, "Hi, my dog is a two year old collie mix and I was wondering how you set it up for a dog walker to come and take her out because I'm going to be working about ten hours a day." Right away you can tell the difference in personalities of the three callers. The first one obviously is concerned about money more than quality. The second could be anybody from a legitimate inquiry to another company checking out the competition. The third is a client that cares about their dog enough to have a conversation with you. In the case of the first two callers, the best thing to do is take a deep breath, answer any direct questions, and then start asking the questions. It's always a good idea to ask the caller where they heard about you.

Chances are they don't really know what to ask so ask them about their dog and their situation at home. If they seem to be short with you still after you have attempted empathy, offer to send them your info kit by mail. Ask them to give you a call after they receive it and have read a bit more about you. Some people sound really tough and critical on the phone. One way to test them to see if you can break their coolness is to right away ask them what kind of dog they have and then ask them the dog's name. Usually you can hear a bit of a smile in their voice when they say their dog's name. Then, use the dog's name during the conversation. "Well, what I'd like to do is send you the info kit. Then you can call me and we could set up a time for the three of us to meet, you, me and Fluffy." Before you hang up, say, "thanks, bye Mary." Using the dog's name in the conversation usually always gets a positive rapport started on the telephone and saying the person's name is polite and shows you're listening.

One of the first questions you should ask the caller is, "what kind of a dog do you have?" Then ask how the dog gets along with other dogs. From the first question you will be able to tell a lot. I am not a breedist, but you can tell a lot about a dog's behaviour when you hear the type of breed it is. Breed characteristics is something you can read and study. Some examples of exuberant dogs are the Dalmatian, Wheaton Terrier, Husky, and the Jack Russell Terrier. You can get yourself a breed book and look up the natural and similar characteristics of certain breeds and be prepared for its personality.

Once you establish that a dog is allowed off leash, ask the owner if the dog is afraid of thunder. Sometimes you get caught at the beginning of a storm and the dog might start to go a little weird. So you need to know what to do.

During the initial visit, you'll be able to tell how the dog might be off leash in the park by how he reacts to you calling his name in the house. I've had dogs completely ignore me, while others would be all over me. Some clients might want you to go with them on a trial walk right then and there. Don't let them take up too much of your time, but go on the walk and watch carefully how the dog reacts to you calling his name. If he's sniffing the ground constantly and ignoring you, he probably isn't going to be great off leash except in a fenced area. He might not always come when called by his owner either. Find this out. I discuss the game of "Keep Away" more in the chapter on Establishing Alpha.

Knowing about training is definitely going to help you become a good dog walker. As for aggressive dogs, unless you have a special interest and the time to work with the dog, don't take an aggressive dog. It's not worth your while. It is possible to turn an aggressive dog into a playful, social dog but you and the owner have to agree on and use the same methods. It comes down to your relationship with the dog. I believe that you need to gain the trust of the dog.

The next thing you want to have ready is your information package. In this you will have reference letters from past clients or if you don't have any, use past employers. Perhaps you have volunteered at an animal shelter or worked part time at a vet clinic. Get a little note from them. Put in some colour copy photos of you and the pets you have taken care of. You can be really creative here. You want to make yourself look good. You want to show that you like animals and treat them well and work hard for them. You will have to create a price list, a break-down of what services you offer, and the price for each. This is up to you. It's your business and you can run it how you like. Start off with a cover or introduction letter. Then go into what you offer. Attach the copied pictures. Include your references. Be creative. Be cute about it. And if you stay sincere about what you say that you will do, then you will be professional and your reputation will grow in a positive manner.

I have included examples of my info kit as a guide for what you can do. You can put it all into a brochure form or a flyer form. However, if you plan to post flyers up around your neigh-bourhood, they might get ripped down or get blown away. There's nothing worse than walking down the street and acci-dentally stepping on your own advertisement. Flyers are better if you can hand them to people. Handing out business cards looks so much nicer and more professional. Business cards make you look serious about your vocation, rather than a piece of printed paper that can get blown away. As for advertising, you can put ads in papers, but still the best way is through word of mouth. It might take a little longer but it's worth it.

If the inquiry for a dog walker is not in the area you service, callers will appreciate it if you recommend another dog walker. Of course, you will want to know the person you're recommending. That is what the Professional Dog walkers Association International is for. By being a member, you will know whom you are recommending and others will recom-mend you.

A word of caution about callers who are negative about other dog walkers and how it can affect you. If you make a comment or agree with the caller's negative comment, it could get back to you somehow and affect your business. Bad mouthing others, whether you know them or not, is not a professional attitude. The best thing to do is turn the conversation back to you. After all, they called you for your service, so talk about that.

Many people want to work for themselves and be their own boss. However, the best thing about running your own pet care business isn't being your own boss or working for yourself, it's being able to work with animals. Sure you may be your own boss, but in fact you do have a boss -a bunch of them. Every client you have is your boss. Running your own business is tough at times. When a client requests, "walk my dog tomorrow," do you say, "sorry, I'm taking the day off". I don't think so. You want to satisfy as many clients as possible so they keep coming back.

Questions for the Inquiring Client on Telephone:

1. *What kind of dog do you have?*
2. *What's your dog's name? (use the dog's name from now on)*
3. *How old is your dog?*
4. *Where are you located?*
5. *Are you looking for walks Monday to Friday?*
6. *What time of day would you like her to get out?*
7. *Does he get along with other dogs?*
8. *Is your dog spayed or neutered?*
9. *Can he go for a group walk with other dogs?*
10. *Does your dog have any off leash training?*

Some Reference Letters:

AUGUST 2, 1996

Dianne,

Great job! Bud and I appreciate the walks. She's a much improved dog. I guess I'll see you again on Wed. August 7th.

Thanks,
Wendy

JUNE 20, 1999

Dianne & Carolyn,

Thanks very much for your care of Trixce over the past two years.

It sure helped to put my mind at rest and made her Canadian Experience much more enjoyable !

Best wishes to you both and may JOG-A-DOG keep on running!

Sincerely,
Gem & Trixce

FEBRUARY 27, 1998

Hi Dianne,

Thanks very much for your help with Kramer and the fish.
I always feel easy when I know your're taking care of things.

Best regards,
Michelle

DECEMBER 1, 1999

To Dianne,

Thank you for being so kind to me and for taking me on all
those walks.
   I hope you have a wonderful Christmas time and lots of
fun celebrating the New Year. I look forward to seeing you
in the new millenniun.

Merry Christmas,
Buddy

Past Newspaper Advertisements:

1992
Responsible adult available to take your dog for a walk at your
request. Occasionally or regularly. Two years experience with references. Call Dianne, *******.

1993
JOG-A-DOG
If your doggie wants to go
Romping in the ice and snow
Call me and we'll do some talking
For a fee, I'll do the walking.
Dianne *******

1998
JOG-A-DOG & PAT-A-CAT
Since 1990. Dedicated to tending to the special needs and requests
of the person and pet. Specializing in sleepover boarding in a home-
away -from home environment. Member of the Professional
Dogwalkers Association, Canadian Association of Professional Pet
Dog Trainers, certificate in Pet First Aid. Bonded and Insured.
For a free info kit, call Dianne Eibner, ******* or E-mail to
jogadog@sympatico.ca

JOG-A-DOG INFORMATION SHEET
Today's Date: _____

Client Name _____ Dog's Name_____

Address _____

Age _____ Breed _____

Phone (res) _____ Sex: Male/Female (circle one)
    (bus) _____ Neutered/Spayed

Cell phone/pager _____

E-Mail _____

Colour & Markings of Dog: _____

_____

Days and times walks are required: _____

_____

Date of Boartding period/drop 0ff and pick up times:

_____

Dog Characteristics: Please state yes or no beside each statement:

Comes when called	_____	Good wth other dogs	_____
Plays with ball	_____	Will go in water	_____
Lkes children	_____	May be given treats	_____
Must be kept on a leash	_____	Loves garbage	_____
May be allowed on furniture	_____	Scared in thunderstorms	_____
Chases joggers/squirrels/cats	_____	Barks at strangers	_____

Dog's Background:
(i.e. Acquired as puppy/from Humaine Society. etc.)

_____

Veterinarian Name: _____

Phone: _____

Friend or neighbour that may be contacted in client's absence or exigency:

Name: _____

Adresss: _____

Phone: _____

Any additional comments or special requirements (ie. feeding schedule/medications/allergies)

_____

_____

_____

Please sign below if you will allow your dog to be transported by car.

Signing below acknowledges that Jog-A-Dog personnel may enter your home for the purpose of picking up/returning your pet and to transport your pet by car. Jog-A-Dog and its personnel shall assume no liability for any illness or injury caused to your pet or to other persons, pets or property. If your pet becomes injured or ill, Jog-A-Dog is hereby authorized to take your pet to the nearest animal care facility and the owner of the pet shall pay such expense

Signature _____

Pager # 378-0295

Thank you for your interest in **JOG-A-DOG** and **PAT-A-CAT**.
Please visit my web site at, www.jogadog.ca or
E-mail jogadog@sympatico.ca

JOG-A-DOG/PAT-A-CAT is dedicated to tending to the special
needs and requests of the person and the pet. We are a business,
however we are flexible and sometimes willing to negotiate. This is
what sets us apart from other pet care companies.

Background information

- Professional Dogwalker since 1990
- Member of Professional Dogwalkers Association
- Member of Canadian Association of Professional Pet Dog Trainers
- Attained Certificate in Pet First Aid.
- Bonded and Insured

JOG-A-DOG offers dogwalks on a regular or periodic basis.

- Regular walks, Monday to Friday, are $15 for one hour.
  Periodic walks are $15 also for one hour
- Weekend walks are $18 for one hour.
- Holidaywalks need to be specified. An extra charge may apply.

We also offer DAY CARE and SLEEPOVERS:

For a day care, you would drop off your dog and pick up at a pre-arranged time.

OR, we can arrange for us to pick up your dog and drop back home. The "day" lasts between 4 to 6 hours. The "day" consists of two walks.

— Day Carecosts are $22 to $30.

A sleepoverconsists of 3 walks a day and your dog would be let out before bedtime, and would have company overnight. Sleepovers provide a home-away-from home environment with lots of activity and TLC.

— Sleepovercosts are $30 to $50 a day

PAT-A-CAT offers daily visits to the cat's home to feed, water, change litter, cuddle and of course, pat. We also offer Kitty Condos, where your cat would have a whole room to live in with windows to look out.

— Daily visits are $10 to $14 each.
— A Kitty Condo costs $16 a day.

JOG-A-DOG/PAT-A-CAT understands that we are entrusted with the responsibility of entering the client's house and caring for the pet. Under no circumstances will we breach that responsibility.

The client should be aware and agree upon that when the regular dog walker becomes ill, a reliable and capable walker under JOG-A-DOG's employ will be sent on there behalf. In most situations you will have met that person beforehand.

Payments are due the last day that services are rendered, (usually Fridays). Please make cheques payable to Dianne Eibner. Cash is also accepted.

It is also in the client's best interest to be aware and understand that there is a fee for cancellation if the walker or company is not notified at least a day in advance. The fee is a charge of $5.00. The same charge applies for payments that are late.

JOG-A-DOG/PAT-A-CAT wishes to stress the importance of care and love that all pets (as well as people) need every day of our lives. We want you to feel confident that JOG-A-DOG/PAT-A-CAT provides your pet with all that on a temporary basis. Ultimately you must be the one to give your pet the time and attention they deserve, after all, for being your best friend.

Thank you

Dianne Eibner

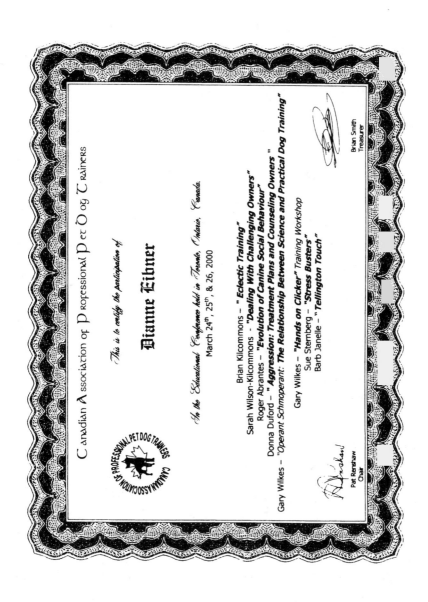

Canadian Association of Professional Pet Dog Trainers

This is to certify the participation of

Dianne Eibner

In the Educational Conference held in Toronto, Ontario, Canada.
March 24th, 25th, & 26, 2000

Brian Kilcommons – *"Eclectic Training"*
Sarah Wilson-Kilcommons - *"Dealing With Challenging Owners"*
Roger Abrantes – *"Evolution of Canine Social Behaviour"*
Donna Duford – *"Aggression: Treatment Plans and Counseling Owners "*
Gary Wilkes – *"Operant Schmoperant: The Relationship Between Science and Practical Dog Training"*

Gary Wilkes – *"Hands on Clicker" Training Workshop*
Sue Sternberg – *"Stress Busters"*
Barb Janelle – *"Tellington Touch"*

Brian Smith
Treasurer

Pat Renshaw
Chair

Your Pet's Happiness is Our Success!

DIANNE EIBNER
1-800-275-0910
Cell: 647-296-DOGS (3647)
www.jogadog.ca
E-mail: jogadog@sympatico.ca

🐾 Dog Walking
🐾 Sleepover Boarding
🐾 Kitty Condos/Visits

Pet First Aid Certified   CCGC Evaluator
Member of PDWAI and CAPPDT

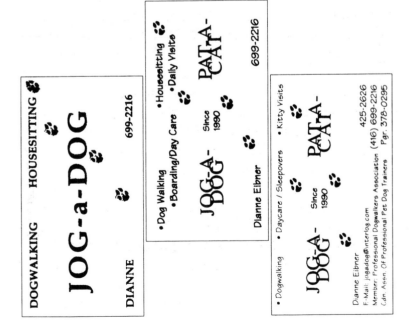

DOGWALKING   HOUSESITTING 🐾

JOG-a-DOG

DIANNE   699-2216

• Dog Walking   • Housesitting 🐾
       • Boarding/Day Care   • Daily Visits

JOG-A-
DOG   Since 1990

PAT-A-
CAT

Dianne Eibner   699-2216

• Dogwalking   • Daycare / Sleepovers   • Kitty Visits

JOG-A-
DOG   Since 1990

PAT-A-
CAT

Dianne Eibner   425-2626
E-Mail: jogadog@interlog.com   (416) 699-2216
Member Professional Dogwalkers Association
Can Assn. Of Professional Pet Dog Trainers   Pgr. 378-0295

Dog Writers Association of America
2000 Writing Competition

Certificate of

Nomination

awarded for excellence in the category of short book to

The Face in the Window
by Dianne Eibner
Jog-A-Dog

Mordecai Siegal, President

P.J. Richardson, Contest Chair

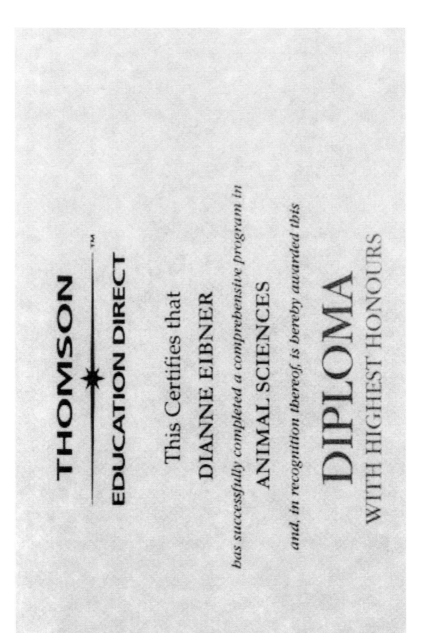

THOMSON™

EDUCATION DIRECT

This Certifies that

DIANNE EIBNER

has successfully completed a comprehensive program in

ANIMAL SCIENCES

and, in recognition thereof, is hereby awarded this

DIPLOMA

WITH HIGHEST HONOURS

LIFE LESSONS LEARNED FROM A DOG:

Leave room in your schedule for a good nap.

Chapter 3

Establishing Alpha

I read that professional trainers establish short cuts to becoming alpha to any dog they meet. They deliver their message with body language, behavior, and an air of confidence. I found these steps in a book called Second-Hand Dog by Carol Lea Benjamin. It can work for professional dog walkers too.

1. **Always praise the dog as if you own him.** Put your hands firmly on the dog. Hug the dog. Pet him so that your hands get warm from the contact. Do not praise in an offhand or timid way.

2. **Praise warmly, well and quickly.** Do not drag out your praising of a working dog. You don't need to fawn over him. He's supposed to listen to you.

3. **Reprimand fairly and quickly, then forgive.** When you put your hands on the dog, do it with confidence and authority. This does not mean hitting. Hands on can mean a collar shake, a leash correction, and a surprising assist into a sit or down. Do it quickly and with authority. Then when you've made the dog do exactly what you want- once- give him a hug. That's alpha.

4. **Give permission.** Give it for what he is about to do any-way as long as it is okay with you. This does not mean you say OK when you see him about to steal your dinner. This means you do say OK when the dog is about to get into the car for a ride with you, eat the food in his bowl, or go out with you for his afternoon walk. In a subtle way you are teaching the dog to look to you for approval and per-mission instead of making decisions on his own. Remember, the better behaved the dog, the more freedom and fun he can have.

5. **Deny permission.** Monitor the dog's behavior. Teach him some manners. Even if the owners like him to walk on the couch and coffee table, he shouldn't behave that way in your or other people's homes. When you take him to the lake he should wait for permission to swim. This can be difficult for a dogwalker if the owners don't monitor and practice this as well. And he should come onto your bed only with permission, too.

6. **Do a sit-stay.** (Carol Lea Benjamin's own) laid back way of becoming alpha in five to ten minutes is to put the dog in a sit-stay. If he's a wild animal and he doesn't know the meaning of the word obedient, all the better. "When he breaks, and he will, I put him back. If he breaks 14 times, I put him back 14 times." At the end of a few minutes, the dog knows you're alpha. And this is with no yelling, no hitting, and no electronic stimulation, no leaving him in the kennel for three days, no nothing. Just a sit-stay. Easy. Effective.

7. **Stand tall.** Use your voice to express your confidence. Act like a top dog -benevolent, but alpha. Tough but

loving. Capable of getting what you want, what's necessary for safety and sanity. Never jerky, show-offy, arbitrarily unfair, sadistic. Never. Can a dog understand what's fair and what isn't? YES.

8. **Be a model to your dog.** The top dog behaves with dignity, surety, confidence, authority, and intelligence. Be like his mother, comfortable in the alpha role. It can help a dog be calm. Comfort is contagious.

The game of "Keep Away" does not necessarily mean that the dog doesn't know what "come" means. "Keep away" is deliberately not coming when called. In that situation, if he's not already wearing a long training lead that drags on the ground, you know next time, he will. Try enticing him with biscuits and toys. Sometimes it works. Don't get mad, but don't laugh either. At times I have tried to get a dog's attention by throwing snow balls at him. I thought perhaps if I could surprise him for a second, I could grab him while he's shaking his head. Don't turn it into a game. If the dog thinks he's playing a game, he will always stay just an arms length out of reach. Ignoring him, is often what really works. Then again it depends on the dog. If you're in a hurry and try ignoring the dog, he'll know if you're rushing and he'll interpret it as a game. I have spent up to 45 minutes with a dog both ignoring and enticing. I talked to the dog and told him about my day and all the things I have to do and how he was holding me up.

Sometimes explaining it to them can help. Other times, I have let the other dogs back out of the car to go and "get him" for me. Sometimes the others can round up a dog for you. What you have to do is get the dog's attention to let him know that you are serious. In time, if you and the owner want to, you could work on that problem with consistent training.

As I mentioned in Chapter 1, Characteristics of Dogs in a Group, taking on an aggressive dog can be time consuming and tedious. Joker, a German Shepherd, was the first dog I ever trained on my instincts. As a pup, I took him out with a few other dogs, then he began to play roughly with other dogs. Not at first, but, I noticed a behavioral problem starting, a few months after I started walking him. He was about 7 months old. I had to stop walking him with the others and walk him on leash with his leash wrapped around my waist, because if he saw another dog, he would lunge at it. Eventually, I couldn't take him out in public at all. I couldn't keep walking like that, and he wasn't getting anything out of it either. So I would play with him in his backyard. What I did was teach him to play fetch. If he snapped at the ball in my hand, I would say "no" in a disappointed and angry tone and quickly and lightly bunt him in the nose with the ball. Then, we'd start over. I praised him when he took the ball "gently." That's how he learned what "no" meant and what "gentle" meant. I'd praise with a happy, smiling voice and would pet him often.

When we had a good relationship established, I started to walk him on the street again. Since he understood some new words and their meanings, we were able to pass by other dogs without a struggle. I wouldn't stand there while the other dog passed by. I kept walking and praised Joker as we passed by quickly and quietly.

Then we started to go to the park. Joker knew we would be playing ball, his favorite game now, so he wasn't interested in bolting towards other dogs anymore. We developed and enjoyed quality time together. Back then, I wasn't sure if what I was doing was completely correct, but it seemed to work. After that, I took Joker to some dog obedience classes and we worked on the basic obedience commands. He was so intelligent. I was able to call out to him to "sit" when he was retrieving the ball, and running back to me he would stop in mid stride to sit for me. Joker was the first dog I taught to do that. Then I started to do it with everyone else. As for breaking Joker's aggression with other dogs, I think we developed a trust between each other when I taught him "no" and "gentle." It was fun for him to learn, because the game fetch was so much fun for us. He liked me, and respected my judgement of who he could and could not play with. Or, to look at it another way, what I would and would not let him do. I was able to give a lot of time to Joker with just the two of us. But if you're out in the park with a group of dogs and you've got a dog that is playing rough, try something that has worked for me. I leash the dog that is playing rough and walk him around the park in a wide circle away from the others for a few minutes. Practice "heel" and "sit" as you walk. This gives the dog a time out and puts you back in control of the dog's behavior.

"When asked how all my dogs get along so
well, I simply say, they are not people."

— D. EIBNER

Chapter 4

The Five Second Rule

It's inevitable. You are going to run into people in the park that want to know everything about you and what you do and they are going to want to talk to you right then and there. This can be good and bad. It is very difficult to have a business conversation in the park because you might feel obliged to give that person your complete attention. This is not good. You need to be looking after and paying attention to your dogs; after all, you are working right now. Some people insist on looking you directly in the eyes. I have said to people, "listen, we can talk, but I can't look at you right now. I have to keep a watch on the dogs." I've had people follow me by stepping in front of me to talk while I kept moving away until finally if I didn't say why I was doing that, the person was going to think something very strange.

When I walk around the park, I'm constantly spinning and turning and walking backwards. Most of the dog owners whom I frequently meet in the park know exactly why I don't look at them. A great way to take focus off you, is to give out your business card and offer to send out an information package. They now have your number and can give you a call with their address. It's a good idea to ask people about their dogs and get them talking. This also shows that you are interested in getting to know their dogs. Most people like to ask about the dogs you have with you. They point out one dog, and you must focus on that dog to answer their questions. You may then become distracted and forget to look at the other dogs. This has happened to me in the past. You are just being polite to the potential client, but one of your dogs is digging a hole or has pooped or is eating something he's not supposed to and you don't notice. That doesn't look good. In order to prevent incidents like that from happening, I have developed the **five second rule**. Look at your dogs every five seconds. Just a quick glance at all of them and you'll be able to catch them at anything before they start. Five seconds is also more than enough time to just nod your head and smile at the potential client and then look back to your dogs.

For instance, you'll notice that it takes longer than 5 seconds for a dog to have a poop, dig a huge hole, run off, or pick something off the ground. Glancing at your dogs every 5 seconds is a sure way to keep them all together with you. **It's all about prevention.** You can have a wonderful job if you're willing to really get to know your dogs and their behavior. It's much more pleasant for everyone when you can predict a dog's behavior and prevent a situation. However, half the time the people for whom you prevented a situation, are completely oblivious to how hard you worked to do so. Did I mention this can be a thankless job? Another reason why I say five seconds, is because if you are looking at the dogs constantly and never take your eyes off of them, then you are probably going to miss seeing someone entering the park at a distance. Perhaps a mother with a couple of small children, or a man with a big hat, or a student with a backpack — things with which you need to know if your dogs have any issues. If you're only looking at them every now and then, and more than five to ten seconds go by, a lot can happen. Again, know your dogs' behavior.

Even when your dogs have their poops, and you are headed to pick up after them, still use the five second rule. Before you crouch down to grab it, take a quick look around at the others to see if any of them are pooping too. And what do you do if you see that one dog is pooping in one corner of a field, and then you see another one starting at the other side of the field? The problem you might run into is that by the time you get to the dog that pooped on the opposite side of the field, you might have a hard time finding it. Here's what you do to prevent that from happening. You will most likely be wearing a couple of leashes around you. Take one off and go to the dog pooping closest to you. Drop the leash on the ground next to the pile of poop, and then run to the dog pooping farthest from you. Then backtrack to the other piles, finding the poop where you have marked the spots. If you bring along a tennis racket, (which I use to hit the balls for the dogs) I suggest using that or leashes, instead of your hat or a mitten, something that can't easily blow away. You might be in a park that has lots of trees or benches; these things can be used as markers too. For instance, instead of running up to mark the spot, just remember that the dog pooped between tree number three and four. You can use a bench or garbage can as a marker too.

The five second rule, I'd like to mention, also applies to the time up to which it should take to reward a dog with a biscuit or verbal praise. If you wait too long, the dog could do some other behavior. Then, it looks (to the dog) like you have just rewarded him for the last thing he did — which might not be what you wanted to encourage. It's all about being perceptive and preventing situations or confrontations in the park.

"We are like shepherds tending to the flock.
Care for them. Respect them. Guide them."

— D. Eibner

Chapter 5

Poop Scooping

You will be able to tell whether you are cut out for this job when you arrive at the house to pick up a dog and her resting quarters are covered in diarrhea. Many, many times I have found myself elbow deep in dog poop. I have picked up dogs that have had clumps of sticky poop stuck to their bum and the fur around it. I have had to wipe dogs down, cut the poop off (along with the fur), and have had to give them full-fledged baths. Let's face it. Shit happens. Are you ready for the mess? Are you willing to go that extra mile? Well that's part of the job. You can't return a dog in that state. You will have to phone the client or leave a note letting them know that their dog was a little irregular today. Suggest feeding the dog some white rice for dinner. That will help to solidify the stool.

Oh yes, Poo, Poop, Shit, Shite, whatever you want to call it, it MUST BE PICKED UP. I may be preaching to the already converted; you may already know the importance of cleaning up after your dogs. There is a skill involved. I can pick up poop with one hand and eat a sandwich with the other, can you? Okay, there's tolerance involved too. Know that you can fit more than one poop in a bag. It saves you bags and it's not messy if done properly. After you've put your hand in the bottom of the bag, you put your hand around the pile of poop, grab it in your hand and turn the bag inside out. Then to pick up another pile, you just fold down the edge of that bag and gather the poop in your hand and use your wrist to "flick it" into the bag. Then there's the two hander poops, so big you have to use two hands to pick it up, and maybe two bags. Soft poops are difficult. You don't want to smear it all over the ground. You want to use your fingers and gently roll it into the palm of your hand in the bag. If done properly you shouldn't smear any of it. Then if there is still some left over on the ground, either pull out the grass (not by the roots) just enough to take it off the surface of the ground. If its diarrhea, you'll probably need two bags. Then there will be a spot left on the ground. Put dirt over it, pull up some grass and put that over it. If its winter, cover the spot with snow. Do I sound a little obsessive? Well I am. There is nothing worse than a professional dog walker that doesn't pick up after the dogs in their care.

It has happened quite often that I have been accused of not picking up and blamed for mess's left in parks. Nothing could be further from the truth. I have a reputation for being very fanatical about poop. In fact, I encourage professional dog walkers to also pick up unrelated poop they come across in the parks. Why? So you don't get falsely accused. It's so easy to blame dog walkers, simply because we have a bunch of dogs with us. Most dog owners only walk 1 or 2 dogs, but dog walkers who walk 4 or 5 dogs are targeted. People assume that we are the cause. Here's an example: I was walking along a nature trail, and some people hadn't picked up after their dogs. As I walked on with my group I was stepping over it and trying to avoid piles right in the middle of the path. Then some people came along walking towards me. As they passed, they had to step over the same piles of poop that I did. From the looks I got, I know they thought my group of dogs left those piles. Never mind that the poop is crusty and old. People who see a pile of poop on the ground and five dogs walking by aren't going to notice that the poop is old and been there a while. They'll just make an assumption. And some will call authorities and report you for not picking up after your dogs. Mind you, while picking up unrelated poop will not guarantee that you will never be falsely accused, it can minimize the chances. Besides, you are doing others a favor as well as yourself.

I feel it is a good idea to always carry a bag of poop with you. If people see you walking with four or five dogs and you are holding a bag of poop they might think, "Hmm, that's good that she picks up." If you're walking along and just finished throwing out all your bags of poop, you know you've cleaned up, but people don't. I have noticed that people will give you a different look when you're walking a group of dogs and carrying a bag of poop or even just having an empty bag in your hand, to show that you have bags handy. You can show them by holding the bag up in the air when you wave and say "Hi!"

So where are you going to get all these bags that you are so prepared with? You could save up grocery bags, "Excuse me, would you triple bag that for me please?" We don't have to do that anymore. I am very particular about the kind of bags I use. I searched for years looking for biodegradable bags to use for my pick ups. I have finally found a wonderful company that supplies environmentally friendly biodegradable bags that I can use for all my poop picking. They are called Scoopies. You can check out the web site at www.Scoopies.com The bags are mitt-shaped, (finally someone made a mitt shaped bag) so they are very easy to slip on and it makes it very convenient in the winter time. You can pick up poop without having to take your gloves off so you won't get frostbite anymore. (I once had to place a bag of warm poop on my hands to cure my frostbite). Scoopies bags are big enough to fit a few poops in as I like to do. This way you save even more bags. They have a nice long sleeve which leaves lots of room to tie them up with no worries of getting poop on the edge of the bag. Scoopies bags come in a compact little box that you can slip on to your belt or your leash to have them handy right when you need them.

The fact that they are biodegradable and will dissolve completely in about 18 months is the main reason why I use these bags. The cost is very reasonable and your supply will last a surprisingly long time. Besides, your purchase would be a business write off so keep your receipt when you buy Scoopies poop bags. Scoopies are available all over the world. I like using Scoopies bags and I recommend them for you too. For more info go to www.Scoopies.com

Chapter 6

Dog Walking Attire vs. The Elements

I'm not going to tell you what you should wear in the spring, summer, or fall, but I will tell you what you ought to be prepared for in the winter and the rain. When we get a heavy snow fall, it's so funny to watch them all hopping around and through the snow. But some of those days are really cold. On these really cold days, I would have them all running around in the park keeping them as busy as possible. After about twenty minutes we would jump back in the car and I would start it up and crank the heat. We would get warmed up for five minutes or so and then we went back outside for another twenty. We would do this for an hour, or until I figured it was long enough. The health of the dogs is the most important factor when dealing with adverse weather conditions.

You'll need a hefty pair of boots, like snowmobile boots. You ought to have lots of pairs of mittens and gloves. Your gloves will get wet. I don't care what anyone says, there is no such thing as waterproof gloves or mitts. Maybe "light sprinkle proof" but nothing is rain- water -or slobber proof. You need something that is warm, comfortable, and easy to slip on and off; you will be taking your gloves off occasionally to pick up poop and unlock doors. So when your mitts get wet, you have another pair to grab from the car. Or, while driving the dogs home, put your mitts on the air vents of the dashboard and turn on the fans with the warm air. By the time you're ready for your next walk, your mitts should be dry.

Sometimes snow will get into your boots. It's also a good idea to bring along an extra pair of socks. You can change at the client's house if you can't make it home between walks. After you change your socks, your boots might be wet. Put a plastic bag over each foot and then stick your foot back in the boot. You ought to have a pair of those rubber-lined rain/wind breaker pants. They are considered waterproof and stay dry for a long time. You will learn what you like as you go. I don't like rain jackets. They are awkward, and when I get in the car I drip all over the seat. It's bad enough on rainy days dealing with a bunch of damp dogs; I don't want to have to worry about toweling myself dry, too. I wear a jacket or coat that absorbs the water, but isn't too heavy when it gets wet. And it might be good to have two coats. I have always bought my winter and rain gear at Goodwill and Salvation Army. You don't want to be wearing really good clothes when you are dogwalking. For warmth, I put on a lot of layers. Turtlenecks are great, double your socks...I think you know what to do.

When it's really hot out, I try to keep them wet. Seek shade wherever you can. Try to walk the dogs through nature trails with lots of trees and bushes that they can go under. Ever wonder why dogs dig holes in the ground and lie in them? Because the ground is cool. You can use something called a wet coat too. It's a cloth that you dampen and drape over the dog's back. It attaches like any winter coat, but it's wet and cool. You can purchase them or make them yourself. I bring a jug of water for drinking and another to pour over them (and you), if needed. Bring two jugs. One that you filled up before you left and the other,that you took out of the freezer that morning. As the day goes on, the ice will slowly melt, ensuring you'll always have some ice cold water on hand. Also in the car, I have attached a drink bottle to the barrier, the type that rabbits use. Some of the dogs have figured out how to use it and can get a drink of water from it. Little roll up bowls made of waterproof fabric are good because you can scrunch them up and put them in your pocket or clip them onto you. The best piece of clothing I bought was my fishing vest. The vest is something you can wear all year round. It has lots of little pockets all over it. I fold up my poop baggies and hide them in every pocket. I also have a lot of other little useful things hidden in that jacket. When you read the chapter about first aid, you'll see why a fishing vest is a good investment. It's light-weight, comes in various styles and you can customize it to suit your needs. I also have several fani-packs. They are small, but can hold a lot. I bought one from Neo-Paws, which has been very useful especially when it's really hot. I don't want to carry around a lot of weight in the heat. Another useful hint: get yourself a hand towel and attach it to your belt; when the dog brings you back a slobbery, wet ball, you can wipe your hands off on the towel. Don't forget your sunscreen and make sure the dogs don't lick it all off you.

I don't advise wearing headphones while you walk. It can be a distraction from your job watching the dogs. It's best if you hear and listen to the sounds of the dogs playing, because their sounds can change quickly and become serious if and when a fight breaks out. If you can hear it, you should be able to foresee it and prevent it.

One little thing I wanted to mention is that I try to keep my finger nails clipped short so that dirt can't build up under them. I find when my nails are long and I carry dirt under them, it increases my chances of getting sick. I don't want that so I keep my nails short. It works for me.

The walk is going to be much more pleasant for you and everyone else if you are comfortable. You will enjoy your job more if you are prepared for the weather, and in turn you will do a better job. Remember, weather plays a big part in professional dog walking, so if you're bothered by the elements, perhaps this isn't for you.

Chapter 7

What a Dogwalkers' Car Should Have

A dog walker's car can be a place of sanctuary if it has in it the things that you need. For instance, you will need different things in your car at various times of the year. But it's always good to have lots of towels and blankets to line the seats of your car. Old t-shirts make great seat covers for the back of the seat. Another neat trick is to stuff a tissue box full of bags and secure it to the dashboard where they are always on hand. I always have an extra leash, a plastic container(such as a margarine container) with lid, a rope with a clip on the end (to use as a long training lead), a muzzle and a head halter, a water bottle, some paper and a pen, tennis balls or other toys, a tennis racket and a flashlight.

A First Aid Kit

You don't have to go through a first aid course to know that just having some of these things in the car is going to be useful for things other than injuries. These aren't in any sort of order, but this is what I've found helpful at times:

Lots of water
Tissues

Scissors
A whistle or clicker (if you know how to use it)
Clean rags or felt like material (for a bandage wrap)
Vet wrap – ask the vet if you may purchase some or try,
seran wrap to make it stick
A tensor bandage
Bandages (for you too)
Rubber bands
A bandana
A diaper pin
Gauze pads, and maxi pads and panty liners
Duct tape
A can of WD40 for stiff locks
Anti-Bacterial waterless hand gel
Corn starch - it helps stop nails that are bleeding from
splitting
Dog booties - a good second prevention to opening a cut
on a paw
Hydrogen peroxide
Some latex gloves
Baby wipes (they come in anti-bacterial form)
Tweezers
Antiseptic ointment
A first aid reference guide (to obtain one call
1-800-298-1152 or take a first aid course)
A client phone book with their home and work and vet
numbers.

I put some of this stuff into another little bag that zips or in plastic containers so it all stays clean. Putting all this stuff in a tool box makes a great organizer. Another really good book to have on hand is the *Doctor's Book of Home Remedies For Dogs and Cats.*

Your Keys

The system I have found useful, is to mark the key with some masking tape and write the dog's initials on it. Another way is to color coordinate them with a reference sheet or to number coordinate them with a reference sheet. Depending on how many you have, you can make up your own comfortable system. It is a good idea to get doubles cut of the keys. You should always be aware of your keys. Whenever you think of a dog, you should think "keys." When you pick a dog up and put him back, before you set off to get him, say out loud, "keys." When you make arrangements for someone else to pick up a dog, think "keys". No matter what or how you decide to do things, your keys should be on your mind. Keep your keys out of sight in a container-preferably one that locks-under your seat. Having keys to clients' houses can come in handier than you might think. I have had a few clients call me in a panic because they had locked themselves out. So I would go to the house and let them in. The next door neighbour at my mother's old house was always getting locked out and coming over to be let in. I found it nice that the clients thought of us when they needed help.

There are a lot of good things about having keys to people's houses and a lot of responsibility too. And even though you would never enter a client's house at a time when you were not scheduled, you do have the opportunity to get to a safe place if you or a dog is in danger. Whatever the situation, the client would probably understand and want to help you. Not everyone has these privileges and this is the kind of relationship you want to have with your clients.

LIFE LESSONS LEARNED FROM A DOG:

If it's not wet and sloppy, it's not a real kiss.

Chapter 8

What To Do If A Dog Goes Missing

If, all of a sudden, you notice that one of your dogs is missing from the group, stop walking any farther. Start calling the dog's name. Don't panic. Call the dog with a happy energetic tone. Now is the time to use "cookie," "biscuit" or "treat." He could be just chewing on a stick somewhere a few feet behind you, or ahead of you meeting up with another dog. As mentioned, don't panic. Start to backtrack when he doesn't surface after calling him a few times. You might want to leash the others in case they get scared from feeling your anxiety or from the tone of your voice. Still, try to keep it light. I have had some dogs disappear and found them hanging around back at the car. They knew I'd eventually show up back there.

After fifteen minutes if there is no sign of return then you should end the walk with the others and start actions to look for and find the missing dog. Put the others in the car and go back and walk or jog through the grounds calling the dog's name. If the dog still hasn't returned and it's been over a half an hour, most likely someone has picked him up or he's travelling by himself, perhaps going home. Start driving around the park and on the side streets. Drive in the direction of the dog's home — you might see him walking on the sidewalk. If it's been an hour, you should call the Humane Society or local shelter responsible for taking reports on lost and found animals. Give them a full description of what the dog looks like, his name, the area and intersection from where he went missing and the time it happened. Give them your name and number and an alternative number in case you are not able to receive a call.

Not enough people know to report lost and found dogs to the Humane Society. Some people like to keep dogs and play with them for a few hours before they realize that someone out there could be having a cardiac arrest. Most people think to call Animal Services. It used to be that they would tell you to report it to the Humane Society, but now may be more helpful since promoting certain licensing campaigns. As long as the dog gets reported as found and you report it as lost then they can match you up and you can be reunited. If the dog is wearing a rabies tag, the person will call the number on the tag and using the ID number, get connected with the dog's veterinarian. From there, the vet should take their name and number and call the owner and give them the information so that the dog can be returned. If all goes smoothly the whole thing could be wrapped up in a few hours.

Always keep a list of your dogs' veterinarians. You can phone the appropriate clinic to find out if anyone has found the missing dog. You must make sure that your clients have proper tags on their dogs. You could also put a tag on the dogs with your name and number. You can't have enough contact names on the dog. If the owner has gone away and you are looking after their dog then having your name and number on the dog is a very good idea.

Sometimes, owners put their home phone number on a tag. So then, if someone finds the dog, they will call the number and leave a message at the house. But if you're not staying at the owner's house, you can't get the message. Ask the owners to show you how to work their answering machine or service.

Most of the time, a nice person will pick up a lost dog. Nevertheless, it is important that everyone knows how to report a missing dog and to leave his or her name and number. Also, it is very important to have the owner's work number. If an owner is away, make sure you have a contact number of one of their friends or family members so you can get more help. Buy yourself a pocket phone book and put all your clients' home and work numbers in it. I always listed them by the dog's name. I find it easiest to remember who's who that way. Dogs' names are always easier to remember than people's names.

When you are calling the dog's name in the park during the first fifteen minutes, you might encounter other people. It's up to you if you want to ask them for help. I suggest, you only ask if you trust them. Otherwise, they could use the incident against you. It's unfortunate, but some people like to gossip and will enjoy telling other people a good story about how you lost a dog. Chances are, it will get exaggerated down the line, and who knows what people will say about you then. So be careful whom you ask for assistance. Ultimately, you can solve the problem on your own.

These things happen and are sometimes hard to prevent. Be prepared by putting your phone number on the dogs and by telling people how to call in and report lost and found dogs and to make sure they leave their name and number.

I had a little dog stray from the group one time and he was just a few feet away from the park at a nearby house. A very nice family saw him, picked him up and took him inside for the whole afternoon. They didn't know about calling in and reporting the dog. They did, however, post signs in the area about finding a dog. I got him back by driving by the house. I saw the kids playing with him on their lawn. He was having the time of his life.

If a dog is lost and a day or more goes by, definitely put an advertisement in some local papers, make signs with a colour

copy picture, and even put an enlarged sign in your car —
someone might see it and recognize the dog.

Carolyn, my mother, had found a dog running loose on the
street. In fact she almost hit him with her car. She stopped and
asked a passerby to grab hold of the dog. She went over and
took the dog off the street and into her car. The dog seemed
fine with all of this and was enjoying the ride. A few hours later
that day, after reporting the dog to the Humane Society as
found, we drove around the area where she had found him. We
were looking for somebody with a dog that we could ask to see
if they would recognize him. Suddenly we saw a girl with a dog
and we asked her if she had seen this dog before. She mentioned that the people in a nearby house recently bought a lab
puppy and maybe it was theirs. So on a whim, we went to that
house and we couldn't believe it but it WAS their puppy. It
turned out to be a happy ending, and we may have a new client
in the future.

LIFE LESSONS LEARNED FROM A DOG:

Don't go out without I.D.

Chapter 9

Driving Tips

I must mention a few things about driving around with dogs in the car. Never be in a hurry. No matter what the situation is or what other drivers say to you. I had this guy in a pickup truck try to pass me on the left hand side as I was trying to make a left hand turn. Apparently I didn't make my turn fast enough and he cut out in front of me. He almost caused an accident. I made my turn and he fell back behind me. Then he cut out in front of me, slammed on his brakes, stopped his car in the middle of the road, got out and started towards me. I locked my doors. He yelled at me that he was in a hurry and couldn't wait all day for me to make my turn and I was probably too busy talking to my dogs.

I wonder if driver's with those Baby on Board signs ever get yelled at or get told to hurry up. I have just as precious a cargo and often that is not recognized. I always let other drivers in before me, especially if I see they have a dog in their car. But since that episode — and a few others — I have gotten my windows tinted. Now, I don't have as many problems with people and their weird looks. On the other hand, when the dogs have their heads stuck out the windows and their tongues are half way touching the ground, I do get many people smiling and pointing at my car.

Be a courteous driver. There are too many jerks out there. There are too many stupid people out there, too. I have some driving tips that I think will help drivers communicate with each other. If you think they are good then please tell your friends and family about it and maybe we can start to clean up the roads. I think that drivers should use their headlights more to communicate with other drivers. I always do this. A series of quick flashes tells the other driver to go and one flash says thank you to the other driver for letting me go. Flashing your lights is better than waving because its quicker, you keep your hands on the wheel, and you are communicating silently. Honking your horn can be misinterpreted as pushy or rude or obnoxious and shouting out your window nowadays — forget it.

Another thing to know, if you're driving along and someone flashes their lights at you it could mean that there is a police car or some obstruction up ahead that you are heading towards.

How about this one: When you're pulling over to the side of the road to stand for a minute, instead of putting on your right turn signal, you put on your four way flashers, your hazard lights. That way others can tell that you are stopped and not making a right hand turn. When you are driving a precious cargo, and you think, "if I go now I think I can make it," then don't go. Instead, wait until you feel confident, comfortable and know for sure, then go. You are carrying a lot of other people's love.

Chapter 10

Employer Beware

Public Relations are important for those who run their own business. If you have employees, stress to them that if there are any problems or concerns, they should be addressed to you, not to the client. Employees are allowed to talk to clients of course, they should have a good relationship with each other and you should have a good relationship with your employees. However, always be aware of when your employee speaks to a client and for what reason. When you lose contact with your client and your employee, you risk losing both. Early on in my business career, an employee decided to start her own dog walking company and befriended my clients whose dogs she was walking for me. She told them that she was branching off on her own and gave them the choice to keep her as their walker or go back to my company and risk getting someone else to walk their dog. I didn't find out until three of my clients asked me for their keys back and said they were going to use her from now on. I confronted my clients and explained to them I was not aware of this choice they had been given. Nonetheless, they would be using this person they had been familiar with over the past few months. She turned out to be rather unreliable anyway, as she left the country and gave the business to someone else to handle.

From then on, I have had employees sign a contract with me. Write one up yourself for protection. I've included an example.

In 2003, another employee went and did the same sort of thing. I took her to Small Claims Court and sued her for breach of contract and theft of clientele which caused loss of income. This was the contract that she signed with me.

JOG – A – DOG COMPANY CONTRACT
CONTRACTUAL AGREEMENT BETWEEN
and Dianne Eibner

NAME: _____

ADDRESS: _____

PHONE: _____ CELL:_____

(1). JOG-A-DOG company contract is valid for one year from the date signed.

You are required to read, understand, abide by and sign the company contract. JOG-A-DOG reserves the right to terminate the contract if any of the following requirements are not met to the company's satisfaction.

(a)   I,   , hereby am aware of and agree upon the rates charged to the client and the amount payable to both myself and to the company in the form of commission payments.

(b)   I understand that I am entrusted with the job of entering the client's house and caring for the pet. Under no circumstances will I breach that trust.

(c)   As a representative of JOG-A-DOG I will maintain the company's best interests at all times. All inquiries, I will refer directly to Dianne Eibner by giving the perspective client a JOG-A-DOG business card with the JOG-A-DOG contact information only. I will not exchange personal phone numbers or other business related contact information with the inquiring party, as such would constitute a conflict of interests. All booking, cancellations and inquiries will be registered through Dianne.

(d)   Once the client has been registered with JOG-A-DOG, the only contact I will have with the client is for the purpose of promoting JOG-A-DOG and to discuss the well being of the client's pet.

(e)   As long as I am a representative of JOG-A-DOG, all clientele acquired throughout the course of my contract is the property of JOG-A-DOG. Upon termination of this agreement and contract, I will not solicit any of JOG-DOG's clientele for 5 years.

(f)   All checks are to be made payable to JOG-A-DOG. If I have any difficulty in regards to collecting checks, I will contact Dianne immediately.

(g)   I agree to conform to the bi-weekly dog walking payment schedule and to confirm all accounts, deposits and paychecks with Dianne at the end of every two-week period.

(h)   If I am unable to make a scheduled walk I will notify Dianne immediately.

I understand that JOG-A-DOG holds no liability for injury or ailment to me caused by dog bites, nips, scratches, or sprains while on the job.

JOG-A-DOG holds no liability for damage caused to my vehicle by dogs or daily business usage.

Please sign below if you agree and will adhere to the testimonies above.

Signature ....

Date ....

Even though I had this woman sign a contract, she breached every single clause. I had an excellent case against her. She fought me on it but in the end settled to pay me the amount of $1,500 with a letter of apology that I made her sign acknowledging her wrong doings. At one point she tried to change the wording of the letter to make it sound as if it was not entirely her fault. So I told my lawyer to tell her "agent" that if she changes anything in the letter she can go to the bank and get another $500 and that will be our settlement. She signed the letter. For me it wasn't so much about the money, but more about her admitting that she did wrong and was dishonest. She only got away with stealing half my clientele. But I discovered a lot of new info about her after she was fired from Jog-a-Dog. My lawyer talked with many of the past clients and we learned that two of them stopped using her to due their dissatisfaction with her. I have since been told that she has been seen walking up to 10 dogs at once and annoying many other park users in the process. She will not be around for much longer if she keeps up that kind of mentality and attitude.

In the midst of preparing my case I called up a past client and asked how things were going. This client had been using the woman I fired. This client had used me for my boarding service in the past and I wanted to say hello. She was very nice to me and she asked me how I was. I told her I was doing fine. She continued to tell me that she had planned to use my boarding service a few weeks ago but had asked the walker if I was available to board dogs still. The walker — the one I fired, told the client that I was not doing boarding anymore and that I sold my farm! Needless to say that cost me a job of about $200.00. I brought this up at the pre-trial and the judge at the pre-trial reminded the woman that people can be subpoenaed and they have to tell the truth in court.

This will give you an idea of what her attitude is like. While in the room during the pre-trial, the judge was speaking to us then all of a sudden a cell phone went off. It was hers. My first thought was, 'What an idiot', but then it gets even better. We were in the pre-trial and in the company of a judge. She then said out loud, "Oh Jesus, I thought I shut that off." That's right — use the Lord's name in vain in front of a judge. As the phone was ringing, she was scrambling to find it. After the first ring and her blasphemy, the judge told her not to answer it. "Don't answer that," he said. By the second ring she was getting closer to finding it. The judge said again, "Don't answer that." Third ring, fourth ring, she has found the phone and has it in hand. The judge said it again, "Don't answer that." She turned her head away from the judge and said, "Hello?" The judge and I shared a moment while we waited for her. Then she said, "Can I call you back, I'm in court…okay bye." The judge looked at me and I looked at him; I knew he sympathized with me. This showed the judge exactly the kind of person I was dealing with.

It was decided by the judge that we were to go outside of the room and were to come back in with an offer to try and settle. I had dropped my claim from over $3,000 to $2,000. She told us that she would not be paying me a cent. Well, it didn't quite turn out that way did it?

I am really glad that I saw the whole case through and even happier that I won. I knew that I would, because even though she tried to make me second guess myself, I knew that I did nothing wrong. I didn't do anything to her that was damaging.

Never let someone get away with stealing from you or lying about you. Set them straight no matter how long it takes. Getting the case prepared was a trying and emotional time because I had clients telling the lawyer all the things, all the lies that the woman I fired had told the clients. The clients really didn't know any better and did not want to get involved too much. I had one client write a great letter for me which we were going to use as evidence. And two other clients that came to court that day to testify if necessary. I had two other witnesses with me as well. One of my past client's who had moved since the firing, had flown in from the States to stand up for me. Sometimes the support you get is so incredibly shocking and wonderful. You will never really know these things unless you speak up and ask. I am forever grateful to her for making the trip.

I have always found that the best, most reliable, responsible, trustworthy, sincere people are retired people. They are mature enough to take your requests and your clients' requests seriously. I rarely employ younger people. I don't recommend that you hire too many people, but it's up to you. I once had five people working for me and found it hectic. It can get stressful and confusing at times because you're dealing with clients in different areas that you don't go to everyday or even at all. Sometimes it can hurt your business. I had one employee who had a light workload, but one day when she was supposed to walk two dogs for me, she called me up late that morning and said that she had a headache. She and the client lived in another part of the city. I said, "could you take something for it?" She told me that she had to lie down for the day and couldn't walk the dogs. I had to phone the clients, explain to them that the walker was ill and apologize for the short notice, but she couldn't make it. You need to be sure that the people you hire are going to make as much effort as you are.

If you get a complaint about one of your employees, then you should offer compensation. That is going to cost you time and/or money. But remember that there are two sides to every story, so listen to both. Afterwards, you will have some decisions to make. I've heard a lot of complaints in the ten years I've been dogwalking. Once, the owner was home and the walker wasn't out with the dog for an hour. Another time, the client said that she paid a certain amount, but the walker said she hadn't. It's difficult to decide what to do. Most of the time when the complaint involves an employee, you may go out of your way to compensate the client. However, much depends on the situation. You might want to terminate both contracts. When I had the money-missing problem where the client said she paid, I ended up giving that client the walks that she said she paid for, at no cost. And after the walks were squared up it was understood that the client would be using another company. I had to go out of my way a little but at least the deal ended in good faith. Sometimes, no matter what compensation you offer, a client won't think it's enough. Whatever the compensation, it's your decision, it's your company, and your reputation. In the end, you may reach a reasonable compromise. I once had a client who always treated me like hired help. I understand that is what I am, but there is a line between acceptance and tolerance.

An employee, a sweet older lady, was walking the client's Schnauzer and somehow, between her and the house cleaner they set off the alarm system. Neither they nor myself had been told of any password or code to cancel the alarm. Later, the client spoke to my employee and was so verbally abusive, made her cry. The next day I called him for a meeting. He was sweet as pie to me. He said, next time, we'll have something planned out. I told him there wasn't going to be a next time and handed him back his key. Then he started to get snippy and said something about learning how to run a business. I just said to him, "it's too bad, I really liked your dog, I just couldn't stand you." He said the feeling was mutual and I left. He was always rude and unappreciative with me. Don't let people take advantage of you or make you feel like you're not important. I know you can't please everyone. You should know that too.

You can't be two places at the same time, so having one or two people to help you is the best way to solve some scheduling problems when your business starts to grow. To choose an employee, you will need to interview them and go with your gut feeling. And remember that you reserve the right to terminate at any time. Decide why you need an employee. Be specific. Find what you want in the person that you hire. Ask for references and check them. Ask for a driver's license number or any other I.D. you think will be helpful. Be friendly, but make sure that you call the shots. This business of working with dogs will sharpen your instincts. Your sixth sense will benefit you.

Chapter 11

All in a Days Work

If you're going to become a dog walker then become a highly respected dog walker. Be sincere about what you say and do. The Professional Dog Walkers Association International was formed so that we could be recognized as individuals and businesses that care about, protect and enhance the community in which we work. When someone sees a dog walker in the park they should be reassured that, that park is getting a once over cleaning. It's being cleaned of dog poop, garbage and other hazards, such as broken glass. You are making the area safe for other people and dogs. Dog walkers as well as dog owners are often falsely accused of being irresponsible. It hurts us more, because we rely on a good reputation to keep us working. We easily become a target or scapegoat, because we have a group of dogs with us. Some people see it as unsightly. Others are scared of dogs. Unfortunately, even a group of well behaved, gentle dogs who are minding their own business, can still be the brunt of some people's frustrations.

This is a wonderful occupation if you don't let people and their opinions get to you. Try never to start a confrontation with anyone you meet in the park. It might be difficult at times, but the best thing to do is not say anything back and walk away with your dogs. This is a chapter dedicated to telling you how nasty and mean and vicious some people can be. You need to know how to deal with them in case you ever come in contact. People, when they have time on their hands, can make your life very difficult and may even try to put you out of business.

"It's 1998 at the end of May. Summer is approaching, and the usual places where I go with my dogs won't be as readily available as they were in the winter, spring and fall. I might even show up at a park with a car full of dogs and have to turn around and go somewhere else, because it's occupied with people that have a permit to be there or just got there first. I have even had to leave a park just a few minutes after I had arrived because it's being taken over by other kinds of park users. I have seen people play ball games in the actual designated off leash dog play area. So I have to gather up my dogs and go elsewhere. Elsewhere is getting more and more scarce. At this time there needs to be more designated dog play areas."

It started off as a game called "fetch." Then it was interpreted as walking your dog off leash. However you want to define it, you are at fault because you are breaking a by-law. If a person is looking out of their window from inside their house and sees you playing fetch with your dog they can call Animal Services and have you charged. This person that was inside their house did not come into any contact with you or your dog. Nonetheless, you are wrong and they are right. Then the designated off-leash area came into effect and you could play fetch with your dog and not be charged with an illegal offence. Now, if you are in a designated area playing fetch and a person walks through the designated area perhaps not realizing it is a designated area, if your dog runs up to that person, drops the ball, and that person gets scared or offended, they could still cause a few problems for you, if they wanted. The person could try to get the area abolished and say that you don't have control of your dog. Of course if he said that the dog tried to bite or barked viciously, it would all be lies, but once that has been said about your dog it is very difficult to appeal that kind of complaint.

So people that have no physical or verbal contact with you can still really mess things up for you. If people want to be mean, they will. It's not just with dogs. But when dealing with the subject of dogs it's just harder to prove the good in your dog. Did you know that if I am walking along the street and I see a house with a fence that looks a little too high, I can call the proper authorities in the City to go and inspect the height of the fence. If it is above the maximum allowable height, I can have that person ordered to cut his fence down to the proper height. That is how the world and the people in it and the system we live by works. Therefore, if you choose dog care as your profession, be sure you have nice people around you wherever you go.

There was a woman who lived at the end of a dead end street near a park frequented by dog owners. Before the Professional Dog Walkers Association International, I helped run a Dog Owners Association. Her name had been on a list of interested people to call for meetings. So I called her up one day and we chatted about the Association and how most of the dogs that went to that park are so friendly and so were the people. But we couldn't figure out why there was still always poop left on the ground when everyone we knew that went there was responsible. Due to some complaints about the poop, there had been rumours that Animal Services was going to start ticketing and we might not be allowed to have our dogs off leash anymore. This woman then said to me, "Well y'know, it's not the dog owners that are ruining it for everyone, it's the dog walkers." I said, "oh really!" She continued to tell me that there are two dog walkers that show up everyday and she sees them because

she is home all day with her baby. This woman told me that
these two dog walkers never pick up after their dogs. I asked her
what they look like and she said that one drives a grey Honda
Wagon Hatchback (that would be my car at the time) and the
other drives a big red jeep (that would be my mother and her
car). I was stunned by the information this woman was giving
me, about me! I played along and asked her if she had actually
seen them not pick up. She said, "Yup, I see them everyday and
they have ten dogs each." "That's a lot of dogs for one person",
I said as I was thinking, about what kind of nerve this lady had
saying this about me. Neither of us has ever taken ten dogs out
on our own. The ratio is usually 5 dogs to 1 person. During the
conversation, I asked her three times about the poop because
that's what really got to me. "So they never pick up?" I asked.
She replied, "Ninety percent of the time, nope." Well, by then
I was about to explode but instead I told her that I'd find out
who these walkers are and have a talk with them. I said thank
you for the information and hung up the phone. I had a lot of
thoughts running through my mind. I wanted to confront her
because she didn't know what she was talking about. But on a
lawyer's advice, instead I told everyone in the park about the
story and this woman's accusations. I collected reference letters
from clients and from people that weren't clients but knew me
from walking in the park. They vouched for me that I do pick
up after my dogs and have only 6 dogs max. with me ever. Now
I have a pile of reference letters that I refer to as ammunition. I
think it's a good idea to document some incidents that occur to
you, good ones and bad.

Here's another example of how easy it is for people to get
misinformed and for rumours to get started. I parked my car to
go into the post office. I had three dogs in the car. When I was
returning, the owner of the car parked next to me was returning
with her son that looked about six years old. The child looked

to my car and saw some dog's heads peeking out of the window. He ran up to my car to get a closer look but stopped when one of the dogs stuck his head out father. He ran screaming back to his mom and told her there were, "five dogs in that car." Now, that incident might seem petty, but I think it's relevant. Imagine how many people might say things like that about you per day.

Here's another good one. I was inside some tennis courts with five dogs. (tennis courts are a popular place to go in the winter time, but I don't recommend it for every park). People like it because it's fenced, not muddy and safe. I had five dogs total after a fellow dog walker friend asked me if I would look after one of her dogs for a moment while she went to get one more dog. I said, "Sure, no problem." Then an older man and his wife were walking by and saw me in there with the dogs. Sometimes they used the courts as well. I knew them from before. We had always exchanged pleasantries. We said hello and smiled at each other. A few minutes later, the dog walker came back to me and the man commented to her in passing "No wonder the tennis courts are always full of shit." My friend told him that Dianne always picks up and she is not the reason that the tennis courts are always full of shit.

When I was informed of this, I gathered up my dogs and headed to the car to go find this couple who had disappeared from the park. I put my dogs in the car and drove around the block. I found them. I pulled my car over and jumped out. I walked up to the man. "Just the person I wanted to talk to," I said. I confronted him, told him what I was told, and said that I don't say untruths about him and his dog and I would appreciate him not spreading untruths about me. There was nothing for him to say. He waved his hands in front of him as if to swat flies, grumbled and then walked away.

Just recently, I had a man tell me how he saw about 30 dogs in this one park and there were three people there with them.

When he named the park I knew he was talking about me. There was no way we had 30 dogs between the three of us. So I told him that who he saw there were my associates and myself and that we actually had 14 dogs there between the three of us. I told him that the ratio of people to dogs is usually 5 dogs to one person. See how easy it is for someone to say something and how quickly it gets out of context. People will go to authorities with this information. So you have to be careful and care about what people say. Most importantly if you get the opportunity to set someone straight, I say do it.

Police Event Report
Saturday July 31, 1999. 10:10 am. Norwood Park.

I took six dogs into Norwood Park and then let them off leash. A man, about six feet tall, heavy set with long blonde hair and a beard with a German Shepherd came in about two minutes after me and unleashed his dog and started to play fetch. Two of my dogs went over to his dog and sniffed him. After a few moments of greetings, the man resumed his fetch game. The Poodle I had with me chased the man's dog while his dog fetched for the ball. The Poodle was following the Shepherd and at one point rubbed his face against the Shepherd as if to try to grab the ball from him but the Shepherd shook him off. The man told me to keep my dogs away from his. I said, "Sure, but don't worry they're all friendly. The Poodle loves to chase, but they're all nice." Then I leashed the Poodle and took him with the others, in the opposite direction.

As I was walking away, he said to me, "I didn't come in here to have my dog play with other dogs". Then he told me that my dogs were out of control that I couldn't control them and I shouldn't be there. I said, "This is a designated off leash area, my dogs are under control and they are all friendly and this place is here for dogs to play together." He said, "This place is not here so dogs can play together it's here for people who want to walk their dogs off leash." I said, "Fine, but my dogs enjoy playing together and they are not bothering you anymore." He said, "You want a dog to play with yours, I'll go get a Pit Bull, bring it back here to play with your dogs." Another woman showed up outside the fence and he told her that my dogs had been attacking his dog and that's why his dog's neck is all wet. (When we arrived in the park, the poodle had taken a drink of water and stuck his whole head in and was dripping wet.) I had the police on my cell phone at that point as he leashed his dog and appeared to be leaving. The police asked me if I wanted someone to come over. I said, "Yes but I think he's leaving now." The police told me to call if he comes back with a Pit Bull. As he was leaving, I heard him telling the woman that my dogs were out of control and attacking his dog.

About five minutes later he came back. He shouted to me over the fence that he was going to bring this up at the next neighbourhood committee meeting. He said he was going to put me out of business, have the leash free area taken away and blame me for it. He asked me for my name and number but I wouldn't give it to him. He said he'd follow me home. He said something like, "You're not a real dog walker. I'll find the company you work for and they'll fire you." Then he pointed to the Doggie Do's and Don'ts sign and asked if I had read it. I told him that I wrote the sign. I asked him if he has some personal problem with me. He said, "I have a problem with people that walk dogs and get paid for it." I said, "Why don't you just get a job yourself and leave me alone." He said, "I have a job, a better job than you." Then he looked at me and said in a degrading tone, "You Dog walker!"

He took his dog home and came back to see me again. He had a pen and paper in his hand. "Give me your name and number," he said. I said, "I am not giving you my name." He said he would copy down my license plate. He said he called Animal Services and they were on the way. He said that Animal Services said, "a little girl shouldn't have six dogs in the park." I told him I was not a little girl. There were other people in the park at this point. Then he walked over to my car and wrote down my license plate number. The other people left before I could explain it to them. As he walked up to my car I was calling the police again. But he walked away and out of the park when I reached the operator. I told her the whole story. The police event number is G135004

This is why having a cell phone is very important. At the least, I recommend getting the pay-as-you-go plan. By the way, I have since collected the names and numbers of nine other dog owners who know of the man who I am talking about and they all vouch for me.

Chapter 12

Paw-litically Correct Ways of Dog Walking

Political correctness is all about pleasing the public by making them think they have not been offended. Offence is a matter of opinion. Still, here are some ways that could help please the public.

When in the park with a group of dogs and one strays, don't call the dog's name over and over again if you know the dog might not come back right away. The more you call, the more it sounds and looks like you have no control over your dog. People will turn their backs when they see the situation is under control — they watch when you are having difficulty. Say things out loud publicly on behalf of your dog so that people will hear and acknowledge that your dog did what you told him to do. When one of your dogs barks at another dog or a person approaching the park and you know that the dog you have is friendly and just vocal at times, you need to make everyone feel comfortable and safe. You can wave to the other person (a universal sign of peace), call out "he's friendly — just likes to talk," or say "thank you, Barclay, thank you" and in saying thank you, you are acknowledging the awareness that you and your dog have of the person approaching. This puts the person approaching more at ease to know that you see him. A dog can make you or break you depending on its behavior. It only takes one dog and one bad incident for people to walk away with a negative opinion of you.

Using "thank you" to tell the dog to stop barking is a more pleasant sounding command than "shut-up," " stop it," or even, "quiet". Besides, dogs are supposed to bark when someone approaches you, so thank them for doing their job. But if you need to use a certain word to make them stop barking, "quiet" is a more pleasant sounding command than "shut-up" or "for the love of God stop it" and even saying "no."

People may associate bad behavior with certain commands. If a dog happens to run up to somebody and you hysterically yell "no" over and over again, you are going to scare the person, they will react, possibly scare the dog and a situation can occur. Having good voice control of the dog is important. Since you may only see this dog for an hour a day five times a week, or even less than that, it can be very difficult to train a dog on that level of consistency. Each dog is different and you will have to adopt special methods in order to gain the control you need.

I imagine a force field circle around me. The dogs should all stay within the boundaries of the circle. If I turn around and start to walk in another direction, the dogs should stay only a few feet behind me before they catch up and are then only a few feet in front of me. They should never break out of the force field. This looks amazing from a distance. Because no matter which way you turn, even without calling them they will follow you. This can take a little time to achieve, but it helps if you touch the dogs a lot during the walk. While they are playing, call them over to you and tell them how good they are and then tell them to go play again and send them off. Incorporate a "biscuit time" as well. Surprise them with a treat. It's good for them to not always know when they are going to get a treat.

In the springtime, when you have four or five wet, muddy dogs to wipe off it gets hectic. Here's what you do. You put half of them in the car and leash the others. Then shut the leash in the car door so the dog can't move. This way you are able to wipe off one dog at a time and the others aren't rolling in a muddy puddle in the meantime. I like to take the towel and loop it under the dog's belly like a sling and while holding either side of the towel rub their belly. This really gets the dirt out and makes you look like you have excellent control of your dogs. Another way to have control when you're walking back to the car with a group, is to use your tennis racket. Loop all the leashes onto the end of the racket so the dogs can walk in a neat, tight group as you grasp hold of the racket handle. I don't do a lot of "on leash" walks for long distances, but the trick to not getting too tangled up is to make sure that the leashes are the exact same length. It's also going to help if you don't have dogs that pull too much and understand "heel".

There are politically correct things you should do when you meet a new client at their house and they are showing you around. Unless they offer, I never ask to be shown all over the house. I ask where the telephone is and maybe where the washroom is. That's all you really need to know. I've had some clients tell me that I can go into the fridge and make a sandwich if I like. I never have, but it's nice to know that I could. Here's an old trick that some people have tried on my first visit to the house for a dogwalk. The client leaves out some change, quarters and dimes, on the floor or lying around on the stairs or a desk. It's a test to see if you'll take anything. I have, in the past, enjoyed the game by adding a couple of pennies or nickels to the pile.

Lastly, when a client is going away and you will be taking care of their dog, either with walks or with overnights, the client is going to worry. Naturally. Don't be afraid to say things to them like, "don't worry," "have a good time," and "everything will be okay." They will really appreciate hearing those words.

Be aware of when to hold your tongue
and when to use it.

Chapter 13

Going That Extra Mile

Having that feeling inside of you that tells you it is worth getting out of bed, is a very important part of running your own business. That willingness and desire to go above and beyond the call of duty. When you work with animals, you should feel there is no limit to what you would do for them. So be prepared to work on holidays and be prepared to work even when you get sick. Holidays can be your busiest time of the year, so you don't want to turn away clients. What if you have a little cold? Do you have a person for back up? Either you get through it or you don't get paid. But if you do ever plan to call in sick, you should try to do it a day or two in advance. I know that's difficult to do, but so is running your own successful business by yourself. You don't want to come off as flaky to your clients, so have some sort of back up plan. Me, I always work. If I get sick, I still go out, but I hire people to meet me in the park to be an extra set of eyes for me while I'm busy sneezing. One of the regular dog owners that you meet in the park might help you out on a specific day, if you request it.

Every day, every single day, be prepared to have somebody say to you, "You've got your hands full!" My reply to those verbal observations of ten years has gone from, "you know it," to "sure do," to "that gets funnier everyday," to simply, "I can handle it." I have had people blatantly question whether I have the ability to handle my dogs. I can't stand the scrutinizing, but sometimes I will give them a demonstration on how well behaved they are and how well they listen to me. They are amazed. Then I demonstrate how we're all going to walk this way now (which is in the opposite direction of that person). Some people are just being nice or perhaps don't mean anything by what they say, but when you hear comments like, "I don't know how you can handle all those dogs," or, "that's a lot of responsibility for one person," for me it's hard not to read into it and it's difficult to respond to.

I know I do a good job and you can do a good job, too. Sometimes pretending that you don't speak English and just smiling and waving is the best thing to do in any situation. Also be prepared to be asked, "Are all those dogs yours?"

When I first started dog walking and only had a few clients, I would walk one dog at a time. One day, I was on my way to walk a little beagle named Betty. I think it had been the third or fourth time I'd walked her, so I did my usual route. The next day, Ann, the owner called me to tell me that her neighbour notified her that someone went into her house and left with her dog. The neighbour said, "She was gone for a whole hour!" Ann laughed about it when she told me. So did I, but I was also taking note that people do watch you.

People also get the wrong impression sometimes when they don't understand dog behaviour and training techniques. Professional Dog Trainers are constantly changing their methods and techniques to suit popular opinion. But they will also tell you that every dog is different and each one needs a method suited to their behavioural problem. For example, choke chains used to be the only way to train a dog to heel. But now choke chains are practically outlawed. You won't find many trainers that will tell you to use a choke chain. Times change, and we should change along with them. Sometimes you need to be firm, but there is no need to hit a dog whether in anger or in fear. It will only confuse and complicate the situation. If you know what you're doing and you have a few trainers that you can call upon to ask questions, that will help you.

I had a client who had a German Shepherd mix that pulled on leash. This dog was so strong that just getting her to the car from the house, I would almost do a face plant and fall down every time. She wore a pinch collar that was too big for her, so when she pulled forward, it didn't do any good. The collar needs to be taut for a proper correction to be effective.

One day, I decided not to let her pull me forward so when she forged ahead I decided to dig in my heels and stand there until she noticed that we weren't going anywhere. Then, as we started to move forward and she forged ahead, I pulled her back to me, pivoted and started to walk in the other direction saying "heel" (and the dog's name). When she forged ahead again, again we changed direction saying "heel." This dog had no idea what heel meant and my arm was being ripped out of its socket, so I decided to give it up. In the midst of doing these "drills," a neighbour had walked by and seen us struggling. The neighbour told the owner that I was hurting the dog. Later on that night while talking to the owner, I told her that it was quite the contrary, but to no avail. The neighbour's opinion meant more than my training efforts and knowledge at that time. I walked that dog one more day and found a note saying to leave the key. You know what? I don't stress over it anymore. I know I could have helped that dog. The owner told me before I started to walk the dog that she hadn't spent the time teaching her as a pup. She openly stated that it was her fault. But that was at the beginning. I walked that dog for a month before I decided to really try to train her to heel. I also asked her to try a head halter but the owner insisted that her dog didn't like them. I guess that dog will always get her way.

To me, going that extra mile or going above and beyond the call of duty means making sure that you are doing a good job, doing it right, and doing your best. But sometimes you run into people that just don't appreciate you no matter what you do for them. Or as in the case above will not believe you are qualified.

I had used three different walkers with this one client all of who had been reliable, on time, trustworthy and good to the dog. He only required walks every third week of the month. We had to change walkers because his dog was very strong and the first two walkers I had couldn't keep up with it. (or their arms couldn't). This client was also usually late in paying. One time, his dog got out of his crate and chewed up some CD's. He called me and was very upset. The walker must have not shut the crate properly we concluded. But she got it right every other time and had been doing so for several weeks. We agreed that he would not have to pay for the entire week's worth of walks. He did use my services again for another couple of weeks but then cancelled one week, then I never heard from him again. I called and left messages but he didn't return the calls.

Fine if he didn't want anymore walks from us but he did owe me $45 worth of dogwalking and I wanted to collect it. I wasn't going to let him get away with it. On my client info sheet, I ask for a phone number of a friend or relative I can contact in their absence. Three months went by and during that time I phoned once a week and sent two letters asking for the money. One letter, I hand delivered to the house and put in the mailbox myself. I did reach him by phone at one point after my letters and he told me that the check was in the mail. After waiting another two weeks, I decided to call the number that was on the info sheet. It was his mother. I kindly explained the situation to her and she told me that she would give him the message. Well a few hours later that night he called me yelling at me for calling his mother. Two days later he came to my apartment with my money. He gave me a big bag of change. Pennies, nickels, dimes, quarters and some dollar coins. He insulted me a few times about where I lived (which was a basement apartment at the time) and then he left. My thoughts were, hey, I got the money from you didn't I? I went through the bag and picked out the dollar coins and quarters and gave the rest to a charity.

For the most part, clients really do appreciate all you do for them. I was doing a cat visit at a house where the kitchen was under construction. There were workers going in and out all day. Spike, the cat, was an outdoor cat so I would put him in at night and out during the day. However, the workers had just used varathane on the kitchen floor and Spike had gotten in during the day. I had no idea how long he'd been inside, but those fumes would kill him if he stayed. I didn't want him to be out all night either, so I scooped him up and took him to my house for the night. The next day I took him back to his home and left him outside for the day. I made a sign for the workers to please not let the cat inside due to the poisonous fumes. Just to be safe, that night I took him back home with me again. The owner came home the following day and was delighted.

I suppose I have done some things that might have been a little far fetched or questionable at times. One time, the door to a house was locked and it shouldn't have been. I had a key for the first door but not the second door. I could see the poor dog in the window looking at me all excited to go for a walk. I felt awful. I couldn't get him out. I scoped all around the house. I found a window. It slid it open and I crawled through. I unlocked the door and took the dog out for his walk! Don't ask me what the neighbours thought of that (I have no idea).

Another part of Going that Extra Mile is simply being organized. You will need a time table or a weekly schedule to keep track. Mine looks like this, below. The rate of pay is calculated for $14 a walk for one dog and $20 for two in the same household.

DOG.	MON.	TUES.	WED.	THURS.	FRI.	SA/SU	AMNT
Fergus	✔	✔	✔	✔	✔		70.00ca
Casey		✔		✔			28.00ch
S & B	✔	✔	✔	✔	✔		100.00ch
Jake		✔	✔	✔			42.00ca
Buddy		✔	✔	✔			42.00ca
Cosmo	✔	—	✔	✔	✔		56.00ch
J & S	✔					—	20.00ca
Jesse	✔		✔		✔		42.00ch
Toby		✔		✔			28.00ca

This method I use with the check marks tells me which dog I am to walk on which days. When there is a line through it that means that day was cancelled. When the amount is circled that means I have received the payment due. You might want to have a method that distinguishes between cash payments and cheques. I highlight the day I have a meeting and then I write it at the bottom of the page. Like this:

Meet Sue and Max 7pm.Tues. 21 Main St 555-7913. Bring info kit.

Then I keep a weekly ledger that breaks down the walks into AM and PM groups. I carry this paper with me all week to help keep track. It looks something like this:

Mon.	Tues
F, S+B	F, Casey, S+B
Cosmo, J+S, Toby	Jake, Bud, Jesse Toby

Wed.	Thurs.
F, S+B	F, S+B, Casey
J, Bud, C, Jes, Toby	Jake, Bud, C, Jes

Fri.
Fergus, S+B,
Cosmo, Jesse,

On a day like Friday, I might ask to walk Fergus a little later and try to do only one group walk of the five.

This next bit is about the bylaws for the City of Toronto. Other rules and laws may apply for different Cities, Provinces and States. A recommendation to limit the number of dogs that a person can walk at a time has been an issue of discussion.

You may own three dogs and four cats but only up to six animals per household in the City of Toronto. Due to the household limit of three dogs, Council tried to pass a bylaw stating that you can only walk three dogs. This first occurred in 1998. Professional dog walkers saw many problems with that sort of limitation.

It would not only lower our income, but limit our availability to clients, and the quality of the walk. I don't think people realize that there is a lot of driving involved in being a professional dog walker. All that driving takes up a lot of time and a lot of money for gas. Having to drive to three different houses to pick up three different dogs, depending on traffic and weather, it can take up to 45 minutes. Most people want their dogs walked in the afternoon. Usually you can map it so that you can pick up a dog that is close to where you can drop off another one back home. Hopefully, the time schedules work out so that you drop off the dog at the end of a morning walk and pick one up for the afternoon walk. Then, some of the dogs will ride in the car with the others but will never go out for a walk together. They only meet to ride in the car. Do they all get along? Pay attention to that sort of thing and put one in the front seat if it helps prevent any tension. Even with the convenience of all the dog's homes being close to each other, there are so many obstacles that you can encounter that will slow you down. It can get long and difficult if you are picking up three or four groups and only walking three dogs each group all day. You'll be back tracking and driving extra trips and going in circles all day. You'll probably be driving longer than you are actually in the park walking dogs.

If you want to accommodate your clients at the time they request, you'll have to cut short the time outside. My complete time for one outing for one group walk usually takes about two hours. A half hour of picking up, an hour in the park and a half hour of putting them back. Sometimes I can go home in between walks to grab a sandwich. Other days, I pack a lunch and drive and eat. I just put my sandwiches in a margarine container or the glove compartment to keep it from being eaten. Anyway, I wouldn't want to have to decrease the amount of time I spend in the park with the dogs. I enjoy giving the dogs an hour, and I think they need it. I would also have to increase my rates for a shorter period of time in order to break even. That doesn't seem fair. So if I have to walk only three dogs at a time I won't be able to accommodate everyone at the times requested and desired. Not to mention, that the dogs wouldn't be seeing their usual playmates.

Furthermore, there are discussions of making professional dog walkers pay to use public parks. They figure this will be done through licensing us. They want to regulate us. The story keeps changing.

As of June 1999, the only bylaw limiting the number of dogs pertained to how many you are allowed to own. In a nut shell, a bylaw limiting the number of dogs a person can walk to a limit of three,was passed by Council without any public notification or consultation. In 2005 the bylaw was just all of a sudden in existence. Apparently it was passed in September of 2004 but was not being enforced right away. When I heard about it, it was from a dog walker that was approached by a parks officer who warned her that she could get a fine for $315 for each additional dog she had more than three.

The PDWAI being based in the City of Toronto was invited by the City Parks Department to participate in a Dogs In Parks Strategy Team. Other dog walkers heard about my invite and got into the meeting where a sub committee was formed to deal with the specific issue of professional dog walking and the concern about the three dog bylaw. I personally made efforts to advise the City on how to regulate dog walkers and my recommendation that the by law should be set at six dogs per person to reflect the industry standard set in 1998. I could not support a licensing system until the City answered the questions I had posed about how a licensing system works. From the first day I asked questions in May 2005 to now January 2006, my questions have not been answered. I was so adamant about getting the necessary information in order for me to make an informed decision; for some reason it annoyed the manager of the Parks department. This was the woman who was in charge of the sub committee and supposed to be creating a dialogue with professional dog walkers so that we could come to some kind of common ground about the by law. She did tell us at the first meeting that she would answer any questions we might have. The City at our first meeting brought up the issue of not being allowed to walk dogs in a park while being paid to do so. I went into the first meeting with an open mind and was optimistic. However, I was spoken to in a most condescending manner. We were told at that meeting that they will have to license dog walkers because "it is a no-no to walk dogs in a park and get paid for it." I asked for clarification on the legalities of that statement but never got any reply. I asked for clarification on the differences of other park users that conduct a business in the park and inquired if these other businesses will be required to pay for a license also. I brought up the example that we used in 1998. If a home based nanny takes 5 or 6 children to the playground at the park and is getting paid by each individual parent then it is the same conduct of business as a dog walker taking 5 or 6 dogs to their designated "playground" (off leash area) who is getting paid by each individual dog owner. I also brought up the fact that we are taking dogs out on behalf of the tax paying client. The taxpayers are paying for the maintenance of the park and professional dog walking businesses pay taxes too. After asking for some legal clarification on the above scenario, the City never brought up licensing again.

At the second meeting they were focused on the criteria that should be met in order to be deemed a professional. They wanted to have a registration system put in place now. But again they wanted us to pay for it and I was insistent that we do not pay the City anything until we would get something beneficial. I understand that money equals binding and I did not want to have any kind of bond with the City unless we knew exactly where it could lead. I was not able to get any answers from the City. The rest of the sub committee members for whatever reasons did not seem to push for answers to the questions I was asking. The manager of the parks department, the chair of the committee expressed her annoyance during the second meeting and in turn the other people in the sub committee felt that my inquires weren't necessary either.

At that second meeting, there was one part where the manager of the parks department was raising her voice at me and even swearing in frustration at both me and my colleague. The manager shouted at me, "You are so against permits." I said, "I'm not against it, I just want my questions answered first." Then the manager of the parks department said, "Get over it." I then asked, "Get over my questions Sandie?" Then the subject was changed. I did not experience any cooperation or unity with the dog walker members of the sub committee or with the City's representatives. In fact someone wrote up an analogy which I found to be way off from the actual events that were taking place. I wrote up my own analogy to clarify the issue. Here's my analogy of what was going on in the sub committee.

> *Picture all of us standing on the edge of a cliff, and we are all wearing blindfolds. We are being told that there is water below us and if we jump it will be wonderful and refreshing for everyone. Everyone is anxious to jump because we have been told how good it will be.*

> *I, however, would like to know how deep the water is before I jump. I would like to know how far down the drop is. I would like to know what is in the water before I jump. But everyone else is just yelling JUMP because we have been told it is wonderful and refreshing. I seem to be thinking ahead.*

> *The cliff is the bylaw, hence the reason why we are standing there.*
> *The blindfolds are the unanswered questions.*
> *The unfamiliar water is the permit.*
> *The City is the ones telling us it is a good thing.*

With the focus now being on registration, one of the criteria suggested to register was for professional dog walkers to have liability insurance. Then it was insisted by the others that there be a distinction between the professional dog walker and the dog owner. It was recommended that professional dog walkers walk six dogs but the dog owner be limited to three. This was recommended by someone in the sub committee who does not walk dogs for a living. I did not give any such recommendation that the dog owner be limited to walking three dogs nor did I agree to it. The City proposed that we pay a $100 registration fee to be allowed to walk more than 3 dogs and up to 6 dogs. Violations which have yet to be determined could result in your registration being revoked and your business being limited to walking 3 dogs therefore restricting your income. I find this registration system to be much the same as a permit system. We have been promised that the money generated from the registrations will go back into the maintenance of the parks. To explain further, the City's proposal would not require a dog walking company that walks a maximum of three dogs at a time to register or obtain insurance. At the meeting when it was asked, "How will this registration system make us more professional?" A member of the east end dog walkers group answered, "We'll be paying $100." I thought that was the best, most ridiculous and yet accurate summary. We were also warned (perhaps threatened) that if we did not accept the proposed $100 fee that this issue could go back to the licensing department and the fee could go up to $1000. I did tell them in writing that I would not support a registration system which at any time, impedes or inhibits the rights and abilities of anyone to conduct business. Some may consider this warning of a possible $1000 increase, to be a good business practice and motivation, however, there are also those who may consider it to be a form of discrimination and extortion, considering it would not be a "no-no" when the dog walker walking three dogs doesn't have insurance or isn't required to register or pay a $100 fee. But I'll let you be the judge.

This system targets the already converted dog walker. I feel that when the complaints do not subside but increase over time, because right now the limit only pertains to City parks, the City will see that the registration system did not work the way they expected it to. Therefore they may have to design a further restrictive system and they will have no choice but to take the dog walkers they have access to and be more stringent with them. This will affect us once again and we could end up paying more for the complaints that we have not caused.

The members of the sub committee should really have been open to discussing our options together as a group of dog walkers. Instead for some reason, they would not meet with me outside of the City meetings. At this point I am trying to arrange a public meeting for Toronto dog walkers to discuss another option to generate income for the parks department. There is a project called Leash-Free Mississauga. It is a combination of parks committees which charge memberships for those that use the leash free parks. With the help of the dog owners, parks stand to make a lot more money. The membership fee is $10 for one dog or $15 for two or more dogs. There are over 300 members for some of these parks and all the monies gathered not only through membership but donations from the public, businesses and planned fund raising events, these parks do very well. So, funds could be raised if all the dog walkers in Toronto asked their clients to have their dog become a member of the park they take that particular dog to. But if this sort of thing is to be a success then ALL dog walkers need to band together and WORK TOGETHER! More info about this system can be found at www.caninefriends.com

Right now as of January of 2006, I do not know yet how things are going to pan out. I may have to let it go and let come what may. I just see it a different way than the others do. I tried my best to make sense where I could not see sense and I tried to point it out to the others. Time will tell who made the right decisions. I am just going to stand my ground and keep my beliefs and then we'll see...

I think the City should be spending time educating people on how to approach dogs and handle them, which is what we in the Professional Dog Walkers Association International do at our own expense. I would like to see the City pass the by law of a maximum of 6 dogs making it illegal for a person to walk more than that amount everywhere and I would like to see the Parks Department implement fines for violations and enforce their own Codes of Conduct. This way the dog owner would not be restricted. There are many dog walkers that are walking more than 6 dogs and up to 20 by themselves. But with a legal limit set they would be forced to re-construct their business. What I also wish is that the City would recognize the efforts that have been made by the PDWAI and endorse our education and training programs that we have going on in the City of Toronto. With that endorsement, it would help make the PDWAI more successful in its mission to educate those who want to enter into this industry and to also educate further those who are established.

It is a struggle to educate the public and make a dog friendly and people friendly image of it all. There are a lot of minds to change. I am in favor of regulating professional dog walkers, but I do not want to reinvent the wheel by having the City decide how to run our business or pay a fee which has no benefit to us. The PDWAI is offering education programs for dog walkers in Toronto and we are a form of registration which is what the City wants. I feel that Certifying is the way to go. I had started to design a course on how to become a professional dog walker then it changed into this book. I still think the course is a good idea and the PDWAI in the City of Toronto has a program called the Dog Walker Mentorship Program™

which is a job shadowing program. It is a bit like an internship which gives you some real hands-on experience. A full course would consist of dog training and studying breed behavior too. These days there are many more resources, I learned a lot of things by myself. More info about the progress of the dog walking issue in Toronto can be found at www.prodogwalker.com

I do recommend reading Carol Lea Benjamin's *Second Hand Dog* and Turid Rugaas – *On Talking Terms With Dogs: Calming Signals*. If you'd like to learn more about cats and their behaviour, I recommend reading Lorena Elke, *If Cats Could Talk - A holistic approach to our feline companions*.

Dogs can be unpredictable but let's take a look at some bite statistics provided by the manager at Toronto Animal Control, 1999. Firstly, it was mentioned that dogs don't usually bite unless provoked. More than 50% of dog bites occur on the owner's property. More than 60% of dogs that bite are on leash. 85% of people bitten knew the dog that bit them. 50% of dog bites occur on the hands and arms. 30% of bites occur on legs. 20% of bites occur on the face. Hands, arms, legs and face — all of these body parts are very much involved in meeting and greeting a dog. A few years ago I spoke with five different trainers to ask the best way for a person to greet a dog. The result was this flyer, entitled, Doggie Do's and Don'ts.

DOGGIE DO'S AND DON'TS
Most dogs are friendly family pets. They come to the park with their owners for the same reason you do; to play and exercise in a safe protected area and to see their friends. Here are some do's and don'ts to remember when approaching dogs:

ALWAYS ASK THE OWNER IF YOU MAY APPROACH AND PET THEIR DOG
• *Never approach a dog who you don't know, who is tied up, behind a fence, or alone.*

- *Ask what the dog's name is.*
- *Let him sniff your hand and fingers to "get to know you."*
- *The dog will most likely sniff or lick you.*
- *Speak to him in a soft, quiet voice and tell him what a good dog he is.*
- *Pet him gently.*

LOOK AT THE DOG'S TAIL
- *If the tail is wagging back and forth he would probably love to be petted.*
- *If the tail is straight up in the air and shaking fast, the dog is anxious and restless. Let him calm down before you approach.*
- *If the tail is tucked under and between his legs, he is scared. Approaching a scared dog might frighten him even more.*

SOME DOGS DON'T LIKE PEOPLE THEY DON'T KNOW
- *Dogs like this will try to avoid contact with strangers.*
- *If the dog backs away, then he is not ready to meet you. Don't force him to.*
- *Never chase after a dog that is trying to avoid you.*

DOGS SHOW THEIR FEAR AND ANGER BY GROWLING AND SNARLING
- *If he growls, snarls, or barks at you, leave the dog alone.*

REMEMBER, DOGS ARE LIVING CREATURES
- *Always be kind and gentle when petting a dog.*
- *Hitting, tail pulling, fur pulling and ear pulling are unpleasant to dogs.*

WHEN YOU'RE FINISHED MEETING AND WANT TO LEAVE
- *Say "Bye, Bye" and slowly walk away.*
- *If you run away suddenly, you may frighten the dog.*

DOGS CAN BE VERY POSSESIVE OF THEIR TOYS OR FOOD
- *Never grab anything, especially food from a dog.*
- *If a dog takes something from you, let the dog's owner retrieve it.*
- *If you have food with you, avoid going near a dog.*

Chapter 14

Media Relations/Marketing

Sometimes I can't wait to be finished for the day and get off of the trail or park before I meet one more person. It sounds awful doesn't it? I think a real secret to good public relations is being able to tell when people are going to be nice and when people are going to be nasty. Confusing the two can result in complete frustration. You try to do the courteous, considerate, proper thing, yet it may be to no avail. There is a bias that exists towards dog owners and I see it escalating steadily towards professional dog walkers. The media does not portray dog related issues in a good light so you need to be prepared for some hostility when meeting all kinds of people in the parks.

The media can really make it difficult for anyone in this kind of profession. At first I thought I could work with them and help make the image of dogs and their owners more likable, friendly and responsible. The Beaches, my community is highly dog populated and I tried submitting articles of stories that I had written about dogs and local dog events. One local Beach newspaper for the Metro area wouldn't print any. They would print stories about dogs that were disrupting people in the park and owners that were not picking up after their dogs and children being scared and traumatized. Soon the Beaches had a reputation of having lots of dogs with lots of irresponsible owners. Then the focus started to sway towards dog walkers. However, by this time the general consensus from the dog owners and walkers had with regards to that newspaper and most media, was that the media thrives on conflicts and therefore that newspaper will always be an anti-good dog newspaper. It is just not interesting enough for the media to cover a story of a bunch of citizens cleaning up a dog park, or holding free training sessions, or doing Canine-Good-Citizen tests or about dogs being blessed in a church. Although, I should mention that the Lakesider did print an article I wrote. Pay no mind and don't waste your time if a certain newspaper won't hear you. Focus on those who will. It will benefit you more in the years to come to have other kinds of media relations on your side.

There are a lot of public relations involved in running your own business. You must do a lot of networking, lobbying, persisting and pacifying. When false accusations arise, and they will, you will have people backing you up. Instead of trying to reach the public masses to show all the good that you do, start with one person at a time. Be kind and generous and courteous to Parks and Recreation workers. You could send letters of reference and information about your new dogwalking company to Animal Services. They are not the bad guys. Send the same sort of thing to your local Councilman and let the other people in the park know what you stand for. Eventually, like the law of Karma, all the good will come back to you.

I have to wonder about some people that I see in parks. There are people out there that look at you suspiciously. I've seen cars pull up and park next to mine. The drivers don't turn the engine off, but just sit there and look out the window towards me as I keep on playing with the dogs. One time a person pulled up his car and parked it then sat there and stared in my direction. When I finished putting all the dogs in the car, the other car started up and drove away. Another time, in the winter, when I was really busy, a man with a really big camera took pictures of me from a distance. I knew he was taking pictures of us because when I started to walk towards him shouting, "Excuse me, are you taking pictures of me?" he turned and walked away from me very fast. I never heard or saw anything more about that, but it was definitely suspicious. Your instincts tell you when something is good or bad. I know it sounds a little crazy but sometimes I feel as if there are spies out there watching. Maybe those people in their cars that sit there and do nothing but look in your direction, are just being entertained by watching. It can be quite a spectacle. I hear people from a distance counting out loud. They say, "How many are there? One, two, three, four, five, six."

Usually they miscalculate, but what can I do, shout from a distance the correct number? No, I don't think so. Occasionally I do hear some comments like, "Wow they are all so well behaved" or, "Look at how they all stay together like that."

The parks that I try to go to usually have some quiet corners in them. I bring all my dogs over to the corner so we are out of way. However, I have still had people walk up to me and right through my group and then just turn around and walk back again to see what will happen, I guess. I have had people follow me when I have made it quite obvious that I am trying to avoid them. I would walk in the opposite direction of them and they would turn and follow back. I have literally run away from children running up to my group of dogs screaming "doggie doggie!" I do this not because my dogs are vicious but because I don't want anything to happen in my last fifteen minutes of the walk. For me these sorts of people show up at that crucial point as I'm finishing up. It gets frustrating because I don't want to cut my dog's walk short, but sometimes I have no choice.

Being a little paranoid can be a good thing. It keeps you on the lookout for anything. The last thing I want to say about relations with the media or other people can be summed up with this next story. I once spoke to a trainer who has an Academy for canines. I wanted to ask him his advice on some books that I should read about on dog training. We had spoken in the past and had been friendly. All of a sudden he mentioned how during his training classes he tells his clients not to hire professional dog walkers because they will ruin all their hard work and training. He finds dog walkers to be irresponsible and unreliable and he would never recommend using one. I said not all of us are like that, and I am certainly not like that. He told me that I was guilty by association then. That was the day I started to write this book. So thank you Mr. Ignorant dog trainer.

Marketing your business has much to do about coming up with original ideas for ways to promote your self. Through the years I've seen a lot of my own ideas duplicated and imitated. Then I realized that marketing is all about taking an existing product or image/idea, changing it, personalizing it and making it look like it was an original concept created by you. So pay attention to what others are doing. See what is working for them. Think about how you can do what they have done, but make it better. Investigate how you can cut some costs to save money too. Fridge magnets can be made out of your business cards by sticking a piece of magnet on the back. I never did take any marketing courses when I was trying to break into the dog walking business. I learned the hard way as usual. I paid attention to the competition.

I would suggest going to pet related trade shows where you can get a booth to advertise your service. Joining professional organizations can help you become aware of those kinds of events to get involved. Have a look at other web sites and see what other's offer. Create products that are useful for people such as pens and notepaper and put your name on it. There are lots of ideas out there these days. Being involved in your community and participating in volunteer events can be a great benefit. One of the things I enjoyed doing was writing some news articles for local papers. Keep your eyes and ears open and do what you like to do in order to keep up with the competition. It's not so difficult to stay in the game when you are really enjoying yourself.

I would recommend purchasing two books on the topic of business and self help from author and friend of mine, Bruno Gideon. One book is called, *Don't Take No for an Answer!* The other is called "Wet Behind the Ears, the Adventures of an Entrepreneur and the Lessons learned." For more info about those books check out his website at www.brunogideon.com

Articles from various newspapers:

SERVICE HELD FOR PETS
By Dianne Eibner
Special to the Lakesider

IF YOU WAITED up Christmas Eve to see if that old wives' tail is true, you know the one about animals having the gift of speech at midnight, then you're in the same spirits as Reverend Ted Davey and the loving owners of eight appreciated pets.

A special Christmas morning service was held at Kingston Road United Church to celebrate the joy that animals bring to us.

Pets in pews
The blessed pets included Lilli, a 12-year-old Doberman/Pit Bull cross, who met everyone with a wag and a kiss, is a very sweet creature belonging to Rev. Ted. Then there was Morgan, a large and playful Rhodesian Ridgeback. Representing the

felines in the crowd was Bear, a beautiful velvet-like black cat. Croy, an anxious and friendly West-Highland Terrier (it was his first church service) attended and seemed happy with the crowd. Jimmy, a German Shepherd/Shelti/Hound mix came for his fourth time with bells on. Skye, the baby of the bunch, a four-month-old Black Lab brought a puppy's energy to the mix. Sunny, a loyal and dignified German Shepherd brought his whole (human) family for the service. Rounding out the crowd was Timber, a guest of mine over the holidays. She's a brown and white Border Collie fly-ball champion. When she heard about the service, she insisted I come to give thanks too.

Dog remembrance
This was Kingston Road United's fifth year acknowledging the comfort that our pets give. There was mention of a dog named Turk that had passed away. He was a fifteen and a half year-old Whippet that had come to past services. We
Reminisced and reassured ourselves that we would see him again someday. Rev. Ted gave a reading that was written by Jimmy's dad, Rod Scott on the theme of the image of God.

In dog we trust
Part of the reading said, "Some cultures imagine God in nature or symbols without disrespect or dishonor. I can imagine God in our dog." I agree. In Godly manner, the dog is faithful, loyal, all forgiving and loves us unconditionally. I must also wonder who came up with the English spelling of the word "dog." I'm sure I'm not the first to imply the likeness between the two. I recently saw a woman wearing a shirt that imaged the kind of sign that indicates where a dog lives. The shirt read: Beware of God. The service concluded with the hymn, Away in a Manger and then the passing of biscuits all around. It was a very different and pleasant experience for me.

I'm quite particular about knowing where I may or may not be welcome with a dog. In fact the church has always been an avid supporter for all creatures great and small. You may have your pet blessed at St. Aidans Church in Toronto usually in October. I'll be there and I'll be at next year's service. Maybe we'll see you there.

Dianne Eibner is a freelance writer living and working in the Beaches. She is a member of the Beaches Association for Responsible Canine-Care. She writes about pet events in the area which are held for the benefit of owners and pets alike. Keep and eye on the Lakesider for upcoming fun.

Dogs need early training

I had to write to say what a refreshing and delightful change it was to see a story in the paper about a dog that was doing good instead of harm. (BMN – Nov. 5th, '96)

The article provided an insight into starting obedience training at an early age. People who have a dog or are thinking about getting a puppy should consider the importance of training and realize that results will not happen instantly. It takes time and tolerance. You are "raising" a new addition to your family. Please teach dogs proper social canine etiquette and let's try to be more tolerant during the learning process. After all, everything was a baby once, even you.

— Dianne Eibner

Can shortage bugs dogwalker

I just wanted to ad a comment to the last letter about dog-walkers needing more trash cans. As a professional dog walker of eight years, I noticed that every winter in the park the number of trash cans decreases.

For some reason, just when we need them the most, they are not there. In the summer I asked for a trash can to be placed in a certain area in a certain park because it does seem prudent to place them at the mouths of the parks. I called a city number and was passed on through 12 different phone numbers from there before I was told of the correct person to ask for such a mission. Then I waited and waited, and the trash can never surfaced. I have always picked up after my dogs and encourage others professional or not to do the same.

Kudos to you if you walk that extra mile to throw out your doggie bag.

— Dianne Eibner

CAPPDT FORUM　　　　　Spring 1999
New member started training without knowing it
By Dianne Eibner

For the past nine years, I've been working with dogs — with other people's dogs. Playing with them mostly, and telling them to "sit" before I give them a treat and "heel" beside me until we get into the park and telling them "no" and "off" and "good dog." I realized this past year that I have been training. I provide a Professional Dog Walking service. Nevertheless, I had been dog training. I don't have a facility, nor do I hold classes to teach, but I have an important role in that I reinforce and "keep up" the hard work that the owners have done with their dogs.

I mean, what would the point be in taking a person's dog out for exercise and socializing if I am going to teach the dogs bad manners? My job wouldn't last very long. Continuing education is the key to a long and successful career. Especially an ever growing, ever changing, ever-popular one like working with dogs. Just like Ian Dunbar said in his puppy training video, "Training never stops." I will have the opportunity to experience the CAPPDT New Wave of Dog Training Conference this March. I can't wait!

For now I have just been able to read books or watch videos but since I took that Pet First Aid Course in the summer, I met at woman who told me about the Canadian Association of Professional Pet Dog Trainers, I have been building my knowledge, skills and confidence at a steady pace. I think it's all about trainers helping dogwalkers helping the owners with their dogs. Why else would you get into this realm of business in the first place. I've always known there is much more to it than just walking another person's dog. It's also about making a difference.

I hope other professional pet care services realize the foundation of their success will be through love of dogs, sincerity to their advertisements and knowledge of dog training. I'm happy to be a part of the circle and happy to be a help.

JOG-A-DOG MOTTO:

"We scoop the poop,
but we don't take any crap."

But I also say:

"Your Pet's Happiness is Our Success!"

Chapter 15

The Professional Dog Walkers
Association International

The idea to form a Professional Dog Walkers Association came to mind in 1997, to serve as a support group and a referral service for Professional Dog Walkers to inquiring clients. After approaching other dog walkers in my area with this idea, I heard about a woman situated at the other end of the City running a professional dog walking service who wanted to start an Association. We combined forces and formed The Professional Dog Walkers Association of Ontario. The demand for membership in other Countries and States was overwhelming and we dropped the "Ontario" part. I have since then been the sole "survivor" to maintain the daily administration of the association. I am the Founder and currently the President of the PDWAI. The association is an incorporated non-profit organization dedicated to the betterment of the professional dog walking industry. We have grown to be international with members from all over the world. While we are often imitated, we have not been duplicated and we have remained the first association for professional dog walkers.

To date, the criteria for membership is to conform by the association's Code of Conduct and Code of Ethics and the limit on the number of dogs walked per professional walker at one time. We require a completed and signed application form, which asks for your business registration number so that we know you are registered with you local government, and we ask for your insurance company and policy number. There is also the contract to sign which states that you will uphold the Codes of Conduct and Ethics and adhere to the bylaws of the association. Upon acceptance for membership you are then mailed a PDWAI Membership Identification Card to carry with you which declares that you are a member and you are a registered business with a minimum of 1 million dollar third party liability insurance.

The industry standard on the number of dogs a dog walker may walk at one time was determined in 1998. Dog walkers came to the meetings that were held when the City of Toronto, at that time, was threatening to pass a by law limiting the number of dogs that a person can walk to three. This would have cut our income in half and forced many companies out of business completely. We stood up to City Hall and fought for our industry and the by law was squashed. Due to the dog walkers combining forces and standing up together, our voices were heard as an association of professionals.

The Professional Dog Walkers Association International will be there for you to network and help you keep your good name once you are established and be an aide in furthering your education of canine behaviour. The information in this book is supposed to help you get you started on the right trail. Our aim is to promote professional standards within the industry and promote the role of professional dog walkers in accordance with the Association's Code of Conduct and Code of Ethics.

If you would like more information about the Canadian Association of Professional Pet Dog Trainers, please call the CAPPDT: 1-877-748-7829 or visit their website at www.cappdt.ca

For more information about the PDWAI visit the website at
www.prodogwalker.com or at www.pdwai.com

Chapter 16

Cindy and Snow

Snow died on Oct. 4th,1998 around 10:30 pm. At least, that is when I got the call from Sharon, her owner, on that Sunday night. Even though it has been years since her sister died, I remember how I found her on the floor like it was yesterday. She was collapsed on the floor, lying in a pool of her urine and her head and back legs were flat out on the floor.

I was a little late getting to the Sheepdogs that day. About thirty minutes later than usual. A week before, Cindy had gone blind in one eye, but was starting to get better. The day before it happened she was running and chasing a ball like nothing was bothering her. Then she had a complete change around the next day.

When I walked in and saw her I knew right away. Snow was jumping around and barking and stepping in the urine. I threw a towel down on the puddle and knelt in front of Cindy. Her eyes were closed but they moved slightly when I said her name. I slid my hand under her chin to lift her head. It felt so heavy. I put her head down again. I felt like I was starting to panic. I called my mother and got the answering machine and left a message. "I found Cindy on the floor, I think this is it. I'm going to Kew Beach Vet." Then I called Sharon, the owner, at work and her secretary said that she was on lunch. I left a message that I needed to speak to Sharon about her dog. I asked if she knew the restaurant that Sharon went to and then just told her that I am taking her dog to the Vet because she's dying. Then I called the Vet's and they said to bring her in. I called Sharon's work again to ask them to get in touch with her Vet. I did all these phone calls in about two minutes. Now, I had to get Cindy into the car.

I knew that Cindy wasn't going to be able to get up. I grabbed a towel from my car, and started to try to slip it under her body. She was so heavy, I could only get it under her back legs.

There were some guys next door that were doing some construction work, so I asked one of the guys to help me carry the dog into the car. I guess I really didn't give him a choice. I'm sure by the tone of my voice and my look he wasn't about to

Cindy and Snow.

dispute. Together, we slipped the towel under her entire body and he grabbed one end of the towel and I grabbed the other and like a stretcher we carried her out. Before that, I got into my car and turned it around, so the hatchback was in the driveway first. I backed the car as far up to the porch as I could to make it level with the inside of the car. We had her body half in the car as I jumped into the back of the car and pulled her inside the rest of the way. Poor Snow was standing beside the car watching all this. I had the German Shepherd, Joker, with me that day, and I put him in the front seat. I had to tell Snow I was sorry but we couldn't go out right now. I put her back inside and she didn't even get a chance to pee. I think back on it and realized that Snow had watched me take Cindy away. Snow and I looked differently at each other from then on, or at least that is what I felt. I had to drive Joker home, he just lived around the corner. A friend was at the house and I remember I said, "I can't walk Joker today, Cindy, the Sheepdog, is dying and I have to go the Vets right away." The woman at the house just said, "Oh, okay." The drive to the Vet's seemed like it took an eternity. I was talking to Cindy in the car but I was crying, too. I was driving so carefully and thinking, I've got to stop crying, so I can see, so I can get there.

When I got there, I parked illegally, of course. I ran in and said that Cindy was here. A woman came out and carried Cindy inside. They hooked her up to an intervenes as she lay on the table. Sharon was notified and was on her way. I went back to let Snow out. I sat on the grass with Snow in the park and she was very cuddly with me. She was rolling around on the ground and putting her head in my lap. I spoke to her and told her that Cindy wasn't going to be coming back. Snow kept on pawing at me and so I kept on petting her. We sat there together for over a half an hour. I put Snow back inside her house, kissed her and went back to the Vet's.

At the Vet's, Cindy was just lying on the table, and when I spoke to her, she would raise her eyebrows. She was very alert. Sharon arrived shortly after I got back and she went in to see Cindy. Everybody was crying at this point. We all knew she had to be euthanized.

My mother had met me at the Vet's before Sharon got there. She had dogs to walk but dropped them off back at her house and came straight to meet me when she heard the message. "At that point you just drop everything and go," she said to me. When Sharon got there, she had to make the final decision. I did not go in the room when they gave her the needles. But I did say goodbye and I kissed Cindy on the nose and left the room. Sharon stayed in the room with Cindy until it was all over. She came out of the room crying. I felt really empty and I really wanted to leave so I could get in my car and sob. My mother and I both hugged Sharon. Then there was nothing to do but leave. It was all over now.

That was a hell of an experience for me. I knew it was going to happen sometime soon, but I didn't think that I would find her and have to take her to be put down. So I thought when Snow dies, I'll be really prepared and ready for it. It doesn't work that way either, although I didn't cry as much when Snow died as I did with Cindy. I remember I would be walking or in my car and I would think about Cindy and all of a sudden just start crying. I couldn't control it when it would come. It hit me hard and happened about four times during the next two weeks. I started to do day care with Snow the day after Cindy died. Snow became a very special dog to me. We developed such a strong bond. But there was something in her eyes that always made me feel as if she somehow slightly resented me. She knew I loved her. But she always kept it in mind that I took Cindy away. We would look at each other sometimes and I probably shouldn't have, but once I said Cindy's name to Snow. I asked Snow if she missed Cindy. Snow's ears went up and she just blinked her eyes at me and then put her head down to rest again.

I believe she knew exactly what I was talking about. Therefore, I believe that she knew I didn't purposely take Cindy away from her, because I told her so. Both Cindy and Snow will always have a special place in my heart. I met them and they changed my life. In fact, they started my life. I tell ya, dogs are just little Gods, spelled backwards.

Dianne and Snow.

PART TWO

Out, Standing in My Field
A Guide to Home Boarding

Introduction

Out, Standing in My Field

Have you ever heard of that metaphor where the events of your life are compared to what is happening with the way an inanimate object operates? I've heard that the way your car operates, could reflect what is going on in your life.

I had been having some difficulty getting into the right mind set to begin the writing for this second edition. Something always seemed to get in my way to prevent me from getting started. One day when I finally decided I was going to get a move on here and put this project together, my car died. Just as I was trying to drive from one place to another, I was in fact, (metaphorically speaking) trying to get from one place to another in my mind by starting this book. After making a few frantic calls to my mechanic and then to my boyfriend, with coaching, I managed to get the car going and got it to the shop. It was diagnosed that the part I needed replaced on my car was called…"a starter!" Hmm, was this a sign or just a coincidence?

It took me a bit longer than I expected to finsih writing this second edition, *Out, Standing In My Field – A Guide To Home Boarding*. I have now after 5 years of running a home boarding business, completed what I set out to do after moving from the City five years ago.

Many other events in my life affected me for a while. Even though I can't really blame them for my procrastinating, I feel that there were obstacles preventing me from doing this sooner than I planned to. I can say that I have now overcome my obstacles.

Setting your priorities straight can be so hard to do but if you want to get things done whether it is to help others or help yourself, you just have to sometimes say no to the things that aren't as pressing as they seem. Determine what's truly important.

There are certain thoughts I have when people say to me, " what a wonderful job you have, so stress free, to work for yourself and to hang out with dogs all day must be just paradise." I've even heard some say that my job must be easy. My boyfriend once said to me, "Have you collected all your hardly earned money?" He only said that to me once.

I feel having transitioned from the daily grind of professional dog walking (which I did for about 10 years to now), that this pace of work is more of a lifestyle.

When I started professional dog walking one of the greatest struggles was having my job taken seriously by those who didn't understand it. I have proved that my job requires many skills, experience and knowledge of dogs and their behavior. This was something that was developed through time. Certain knowledge can be achieved from books and seminars but there is something else you must possess that one cannot learn. That something is the commitment it takes to run your own business.

If you don't commit to what you are doing then, why are you doing it? People rely on you in the pet care business. This might not sound right, but the way it goes is, the client could cancel on you last minute and that is fine with them, but for you to cancel on them without sufficient notice or without helping to find someone to cover for you, is unreliable.

When you care about others, the struggle of whether or not you will be taken seriously will diminish. Honestly, there are so many other companies out there nowadays -the competition is thick. You cannot dwell on the fact that there is another pet care company right down the street from you. This has always been a very personalized realm of business and the client will choose you if they like you. I would suggest checking out what the competition is charging and offering in services versus what you plan to offer and charge. These days for me, it's not even about getting ahead of the rest of the game; it's about staying in the game. If you really want to get in to this business and stay in it, then you will make sure that you keep your commitments and promises to the client.

In this second edition of *The Face in the Window – A Guide to Professional Dog Walking*, with the addition of *Out, Standing in My Field – A Guide to Home Boarding*, I will discuss the decisions that you will have to make and the effects they will have on your life. If you are indeed set on running a home boarding business, you will see what it really entails and how much time, effort and sacrifice it truly takes on your life.

This is what running your own business is about. Making decisions and sticking to your word. You can change your mind about things but always mean what you say and do what you say you are going to do. This business of boarding, I call them sleepovers, is more personal than other types of self-employment. You will have under your care the living, breathing, "member of one's family" in your home. I will share with you how I have made home boarding into a successful business that you can do yourself on a small scale or on a larger scale, keeping in mind the safety of the animals first. I cannot stress enough how you have to be prepared to alter your lifestyle and make some sacrifices when you decide to go into this type of business. If you're going to choose this type of work for yourself, you have to want to be "outstanding in your field."

Out on a walk in the field.

Chapter 1

Way of Life Business

My dream was to open the front door of my house, let the dogs out and run along with them up to my field. I thought wouldn't it be great if I could do that? Five years later, I made it happen!

I wake up every morning to a big wet tongue sliding across my face. No, I'm not a newlywed, I'm a dog sitter.

Have you ever lived with more than one or two dogs at a time? Were those dogs your own? When starting to board other people's dogs in your home, you will need to take into consideration many factors. Since these dogs are not yours, they won't be accustomed to you or your home therefore this situation could be a bit weird for the dog. There are certain questions to ask before you take this dog on as a client, and of course you will want to meet them beforehand.

If you have started a dog walking company and are at the point where you want to offer boarding to your current client's, then you have an advantage in that the dog is already comfortable with you. If you want to expand further and interview clients with dogs you have not met, then you will need to have a protocol in order. Not to mention you will have to have a very good sense of how to read a dog's body language and temperament as well as reading the owner of the dog. I have had to say no once or twice to a person because I did not think that their dog would fit in. If I think a dog is a bit aggressive then I cannot take the chance.

There is a form I ask my client's to fill out, just like the dog walking form but for boarding. Many of the same questions and info are on it but it gives some insight into what the dog would be like sleeping over at my house. However, you find out more things about the dog once he is actually with you. There are so many things that you will discover about the dog which are not mentioned on the form or that the owner did not tell you. The owner may not even know certain things about the dog which you end up discovering and telling the owner. It is a different kind atmosphere for a strange dog when he gets left at a strange place. Each dog acts differently. They usually adapt well and are better behaved. The territory is neutral and the person in charge (you) knows how to handle multiple dogs due to your dog walking experiences.

JOG-A-DOG INFORMATION SHEET FOR BORDERS
Today's Date: _____

Client Name _____ Dog's Name_____

Address _____

Age _____ Breed _____

Phone (res) _____ Sex: Male/Female (circle one)

(bus) _____ Neutered/Spayed

Cell phone/pager _____

E-Mail _____

Colour & Markings of Dog: _____

_____

Date of Boartding: Time of Departure and Time of Return:

_____

Dog Characteristics: Please state YES or NO beside each statement:

Comes when called	_____	Good wth other dogs	_____
Plays with ball and shares well	_____	Crate trained	_____
Must be kept on a leash	_____	Loves garbage/people food	_____
May be allowed on furniture	_____	Scared in thunderstorms	_____
Chases joggers/squirrels/cats/bikes	_____	Barks at strangers	_____
Jumps/climbs/digs holes	_____	May be given treats	_____
Chews/Destructive/counter surfs	_____	Likes children	_____

Dog's Background:
(i.e. Acquired as puppy/from Humaine Society. etc.)

_____

Any other characteristics I should know about:

_____

Veterinarian: Nameof Clinic _____
Phone: _____

Friend or neighbour to contact in client's absence. **Use back of
sheet for # where you will be:**
Name: _____
Phone: _____
Address and/or E-Mail: _____

**Additional comments/requirements Is your dog on flea preven-
tion, medication, or have allergies or a special feeding schedule?**

_____

_____

Has your dog been exposed to Kennel Cough? _____ Use the
back of this sheet if needed.

Signing below acknowledges that Jog-A-Dog personnel may enter
your home for the purpose of picking up/returning your pet and to
transport your pet by car. Jog-A-Dog and its personnel shall assume
no liability for any illness or injury caused to your pet or to other
persons, pets or property. If your pet becomes injured or ill, Jog-A-
Dog is hereby authorized to take your pet to the nearest animal care
facility and the owner of the pet shall pay such expense

Signature _____

    I have created something I call the 12 point inspection
sheet. I created this so that there would not be any discrepan-
cies with regards to the dog's well being while in my care. I
simply wanted a form for which I could take note of how the
dog looked when it came to me. I inspect the dog's outer body
and examine sections of the dog for marks that might already
be there so that if anything does happen to the dog, I will have
an account of any marks he already had before he came to me.
I have only used this method a few times since most people are
not concerned if their dog gets a small scratch due to running
through the bushes or from playing with another dog. It takes
a few minutes to go over the dog but it could be worthwhile if
the owner questions something on the dog when you bring it
back. Sometimes I ask the owner to fill it out and then I go
over it with them afterwards.

JOG-A-DOG   12 Point Inspection Sheet

Dog's name:
Age:
Sex:

I.D. – Tags and Microchip # :

Collar (colour/style):

Weight (rough idea – heavy/slim/average for breed of dog):

Examine and comment on condition of:

1. Ears (clean or waxy):
2. Teeth(yellow,white,tartar)/Muzzle/Nose (pink,black):
3. Eyes (normal/crusty/runny):
4. Front paws, pads and legs:
5. Back paws, pads and legs:
6. Body (check for lumps or bumps):
7. Has Dew claws, any torn/broken claws:
8. Coat/Fur (well groomed or matted):
9. Skin (flaky/dandruff/healthy):
10. Muscles and Joints (Limping or Soreness/Arthritis):
11. Scratches/Scrapes/Scars:
12. Articles and baggage (bowls, leash, toys):

Date:_____ **Signature:**_____

It is important to understand that one should not just jump into boarding dogs in your home if you have no past experience with dog walking. It would be quite dangerous not only for you but for the dogs in your care if you are not well versed in how to handle certain situations.

There was a dog I had at my house whom I met with before they booked with me, yet she was still very shy and nervous of me. When the owners dropped her off, the dog would not come to me and so before they left, I asked them to leave the leash on her. This way I could hold onto the leash and the dog, while they went out the door.

This dog was a Chow breed, and as far as my opinion goes, Chows are cats trapped in dogs bodies. So she was a scared, nervous dog and after the owners left, she didn't want anything to do with me and just sat by the door wanting to be left alone. If I got up to pet her she would run away. I thought there is no way that I can let this dog off leash anywhere. I didn't touch her or try to approach her or look at her for a few hours that night. I did however talk to her all night. I sat on my couch and I did some sewing, I sorted some papers, did my dishes and had the TV on as well. All the while I was talking to her as if I were talking to someone in the room. By the way, I talk to the dogs all the time, they are such good listeners! Every time I got up off the couch to walk across the room, she was very attentive and watched my every move. It was getting late and time to go to bed, so I very carefully approached her. Since she had her leash on her I was able to grab the end of it without getting too close to her. By this time I think she knew I wasn't too much of a threat. I lead her out the back door and into the fenced yard. She let me touch her and pet her lightly now. We were making good progress. I remember that she was the only dog that I had boarding for a few days before anyone else came. That might have contributed to her nervousness. She seemed to like other dogs, and was all around well natured once we got comfortable with each other. I did eventually take her off leash and she would follow me around at my heels. I took her to a fenced in park the first few times as a trial and she turned out to be a very social dog playing well with other dogs and faithful in that she would come when I called her. But boy, she sure was a chicken of a dog when I first met her. I could not help but to give her a nick name. She was a Chow named Ming, and so I called her, "Chicken-Chow-Ming."

I love to come up with "pet names" for the dogs. I board a wonderful black lab named Puck. He is a wonderful spirit except for the fact that he jumps up all the time when he gets excited and sees me. Wouldn't have thought of it until I said it to him, but when I met him and the owner for the first time, the lovable friendly guy that he is, as he is jumping up at me, I found myself saying, "Puck Off!" I think I said "down" after-wards which isn't the proper command for that action. Anyhow, I never pointed it out and I tried not to say it again. Puck is a lovely dog with the usual dopey lab characteristics I like to call him by his full pet name: "Sharp as a hockey Puck."

You will discover so many neat characteristics from the dogs that you care for when they come to live with you. A dog named Michael was fascinated by a large mirror that I had placed against a wall that was by the edge of a doorway. I noticed him starring into it and then walking through the doorway and looking to the back of the wall, which would have been behind the mirror. I believe he was trying to figure out where his reflection was or where "the other dog" was. He repeatedly looked into the mirror and then walked through the doorway looking up and down the back wall which to him would have been the other side, or else through the mirror. I could see he was really thinking hard about it.

The dogs that you board can certainly be a great source of entertainment which you are always learning from. When a dog is dropped off to someone they don't know, they figure out that you are the one taking care of them and so they will latch onto you and want to be around you. When I board dogs, I am home 90% of the time and my living arrangements are so that the dogs are always on the same level of the house with me, usually in the same room. Even when I go to the bathroom, or when I take a shower I see these little noses peeking in at me. I can take a bath, and even though it is hot and steamy in there some dogs really want to be in the room with me. One thing's for sure when you board dogs, you'll never pee alone!

I remember taking a bath at my mom's house, the bathroom was upstairs and we were boarding a dog that had a cast on her front leg. She was all set up downstairs on a big comfy cushion. I was alone in the house and was about to take a bath and relax for a minute. But after I got in the bath I heard this thumping and rustling around and then this repeated heavy sound of, "Click Click, Ka-Thunk! Click Click, Ka-Thunk!" I'm in the house alone, in the bubble bath, hearing this sound that is getting closer and closer! All of a sudden the bathroom door bursts wide open and a great big white German Shepard dog is standing there, panting and holding up her leg in the cast. The determination it must have took for her to get up those stairs to get to me. I guessed that the click click sound was her nails from her other three legs stepping up the stairs and the ka-thunk was her front leg in the cast being heaved up each stair with all her might.

How I got started in this whole business

When I started walking dogs it was in 1990 and by the year 1999, I decided that I wanted to change careers. Of course I still wanted to work with dogs but I wanted to change my pace and my way of life.

You see, I started walking dogs first then slowly I started to board dogs. This was back when I still lived at my mom's house in Toronto and she helped me walk dogs. Our first boarders were due to an emergency situation where the client was having her floors done and realized that she had to get the dogs out due to the smells and fumes being toxic. These were dogs my mom and I knew very well since we walked them on a regular basis. When it worked out so well with these dogs staying over, we told our other dog walking clients that we could take their dog if they went on vacation. They started to ask us and we started to have dogs come sleep over with us. It was fun since we didn't have any pets of our own anymore.

As business grew and as I grew up, I decided to move out on my own. I got a basement apartment, which allowed pets so I was able to do more boarding. A year later, I bought a house. Had to jump through a few hoops with the bank because I was self employed, but I never missed a mortgage payment. In fact my mortgage payments were less than my rent. It was a luxury to have a driveway and a yard! I stayed there for three years. After being in the City all my life and dog walking for 9 years, my dream to retire from the daily grind of dog walking and move to the country to board dogs was a much needed reality. The first place in the country that I ended up buying, I only stayed at for 7 months.

After I moved from the City, it felt great. I made some money on the sale of the other house which I used to fix up the new house. However I soon realized that what I bought was an illusion.

I decided after 4 months that I didn't like living where I was. What a terrible feeling that is. I was in the country but I was still surrounded closely to other people's houses. I was having a hard time running my business. I just didn't have enough space. In fact, if I had a larger group of dogs, I would have to walk them away from civilization. The only way I could do that was to put the dogs in my car and drive around the lake to the forest on the other side. It was about a 15-20 minute drive each way.

Mind you, it was a two hour long walk and I would do that twice a day, sometimes three if I had to. I had a huge back yard (which was part of the illusion) but it wasn't enough when I got really busy and had a group of dogs that really needed to run. I was spending the same amount of money on gas as I was when in the City and I was always worrying about bothering my neighbours.

I started looking for another home. I found it. A 16 acre hobby farm, one half hour further north from where I was. I sold the house, lost a bit of money on the sale from that place to the other one this time but it has proved to be well worth it. I was now able to do what I had dreamed of doing — open up my front door with the dogs and start walking! No leashes or loading up the car. Now we just run up to the field.

It did take about 5 years to get to this place I am at. I made a lot of mistakes that cost me but I have gotten over it, got back on my feet and just kept moving forward. That's all you have to do, as long as you are moving ahead and not staying still. Even if it is a small advance, you have to always be in a better place after every year that passes.

If you do plan to move from the City to the country, I would recommend that you talk to other people who have done it. I learned many things the hard way.

When you move from the City to the country, you can be taken in by the beauty of it all and think that you will be happy in a nice quiet location with tranquil scenery. But if you are not careful to look closely at your surroundings, you might find that things are not really what they seem.

The key element in boarding dogs is having an excellent place to walk them. You are boarding dogs so that they can get more walks than they would if they were staying at home waiting for someone to come and check in on them.

Some questions to ask when you receive a phone call from an inquiry for boarding:

1. What kind of a dog do you have?
   Male/Female/Spayed/Neutered?
2. When are you going away and when are you returning?
3. Does your dog get along well with other dogs?
4. How old is your dog?
5. What is your dog's name?
6. How is your dog off leash?
7. Whereabouts are you located?
8. Has your dog ever been boarded before or stayed overnight away from you?
9. Is it possible for you to drop off your dog or do you need someone to pick up from you?
10. How does your dog travel in the car?

Mention that you would need them to fill out the information sheet which will give you some ideas about the dog's characteristics and some contact info such as vet's phone number, the number for a friend who will be in the City that you could contact in an emergency and the number to where the owners can be reached if need be.

It is very important to get the exact times that your client is coming home. Otherwise you could be waiting all day or all night for the phone to ring and you won't know when someone is going to show up at your door. I have been stranded many times not knowing what is going on for the entire the day and because of that I have not been able to make any other kind of plan whether it be going out to get some groceries or if I had the possibility of visiting a friend. It needs to be established when the client is coming over or if you are to go and pick up, and the time needs to be agreed upon.

Chapter 2

Welcome to My Home

I have cleared space in my house specifically to make room for boarders. The changes that you make are small sacrifices when you consider the damage that could be done if you do not make changes. Boarding dogs in your home is not just a job - it is a lifestyle. This lifestyle must reflect your personality otherwise you will be getting into a business that does not really suit you. If you don't enjoy your job, you are not going to be successful with it and quite frankly you have no right to be caring for people's pets.

I would not advise having little glass china plates or figurines displayed on a shelf in a high traffic area. This is a disaster waiting to happen. I don't have any shelves unless they are placed in a room where no one walks past often. Even then, I don't have anything on the bottom shelf. Most of my wall units or shelves have cupboard doors on the bottom near the floor and then where the shelf is open, I store things higher up. Having clutter around is not going to work when boarding dogs. Things need to be tucked away. Dogs will bump into things and knock them over. Puppy's can get into things you didn't even know you had. Dogs that "counter surf" make a great incentive to keep your counters clear of food and utensils.

Storing And Organizing Your Guest's Baggage
As soon as you get home with the dogs, you bring in all their stuff and sort it out. Sometimes the owners might have labeled everything for you but chances are you will have a bunch of different bags of food, toys, bowls and leashes. You'll want to give back to the owners the same contents that they gave you so best to mark each item with the dog's name on it. I just use some simple masking tape and a big black permanent marker. I put the dog's name on everything that belongs to them. Each bowl is marked with each dog's name and so is their leash, the bag of food and the bag or knapsack that the dog's food came in. I'll even put a piece of masking tape under or on the corner of the dog's bed, if he came with a bed. I have many quilts and comforters that I fold up and put on the floor for my "guests."

If a dog comes with a huge bag of food, I like to put the dog's food into another container. I find if I transfer some food into an easily accessible container that is labeled with the dog's name it makes preparing the meals so much quicker with less chances of spilling kibble. I don't like to have to dig down into each and every bag of dog food to take out 1 scoop. I try to make it as convenient as possible.

I was able to find some used memory foam at a flea market — the kind of foam that was developed by NASA. I found a display model so I got it at a discounted rate. I cut it up and I covered it with a quilt. These make for pretty comfy beds for the dogs! Some owner's like to supply their dog's bed for them to make them "feel more at home." It's funny but what I find happens is when I have three or four dogs here that all have come with their own bed, the dogs end up switching their bed and sleeping on another dog's bed. So the dog's own bed doesn't necessarily help them to feel more at home. I think it is just the atmosphere that you create for them which is going to help them feel comfortable.

As far as the toys that might have come with the dog, I won't always use them. I might have a dog that is destructive and likes to chew up toys so rather than risk the toy being damaged; I'll just keep it tucked away in the dog's bag and not take it out. I use a lot of my own stuffed animals too that I purchase at second hand stores such as Salvation Army. Shopping second hand is the only way to buy dog stuff. After all, you have to consider that the stuff you buy could get damaged or destroyed and eventually it will all wear out. Keep a list of what the dog has come with and make any important notes on the back of the client info sheet so you remember what the dog was like.

Below is a list of materials you will find you need (at the least) when organizing your boarders.

List of materials needed for boarding:
1. *Lots of masking tape*
2. *Big black permanent marker (or a color if you prefer)*
3. *Plastic bowls (I like to use my own)*
4. *Lots of paper towel and tissues*
5. *A measuring cup*
6. *Cupboard space (with doors that can't be opened by dogs)*
7. *Lots of moist disinfectant wipes*
8. *Electrostatic dusting cloths*
9. *Lots of towels*
10. *Lots of quilts and baby blankets (I find the small ones easier to wash)*
11. *Baby gates or some kind of barrier to put across doorways*
12. *Tupperware containers*
13. *Leashes, flat buckle collars, long 20ft. rope*

If the owner of a dog gives you a bowl for their dog, and it has dried food stuck on it, I would wash it and put it away. I prefer to use my own bowls which I rinse out after every meal and then dry before I put the dog's food in it for the next meal. I like to use plastic because they wipe up fast and the masking tape sticks well.

If a dog arrives to board with you and he or she is wearing a choke chain, take it off, label it and put it away. Put another collar on for the time the dog is with you. You will have purchased a bunch of collars from the pet store or a dollar store, so you should have at least one or two really good solid flat buckled collars on hand.

Also having identification on each dog will help if a dog ends up running off. It could happen, so if and when it does, you'll want for whoever finds the dog to contact you preferably. You can get little tags made up with your company name and number on them or there is lots of other little ways you can have your ID on the dog that is more affordable.

One quick thing to do is write your number on a piece of masking tape and tape it to the dog's own tags, then put a piece of clear tape over top of it to preserve it. Then you have to remember to take it off before the dog goes back home. You could also wrap the tape around the dog's collar.

You'll also need some other equipment on hand such as your own leashes and some training devices such as the Halti ™ or Promise Collar ™ and you should definitely have a few different sized muzzles on hand.

My closet and drawers are full of clothes I have bought specifically for the use of my business. I bought my car for the use of my business, and I bought my house because I thought it would serve the best use for my business.

I have covers over all my furniture. Everything is washable. I have to keep a sheet over the top of my bedspread. This is in case a dog jumps up on my bed, I'll have a layer that I can take off and wash easily. I suppose I could just close my bedroom door but I offer a service where the dogs live in a home environment. Ok, wait, I don't want you to think that I let the dogs do whatever they want wherever they want, because cleanliness is always one of my top rules. Not letting dogs on the bed uninvited is another. If one jumps up unexpectedly, you bet he/she is sent off. When dogs do things uninvited such as jump on furniture or take food this needs to be corrected immediately upon arrival in your home. I give an example of how I dealt with a dog that wouldn't get off my bed in Chapter 5. I put layers of blankets or sheets on my furniture so that when a dog has been lying on it for a while and it gets dirty, I can take off the first layer and have a clean cover on the couch right away. Then I can wash the other one and get it ready to go back on as the first layer.

My yard has lots of weeds and tuff grass. I have to keep it watered real well and keep dogs off of it during the spring thaw or on rainy days that have made the ground soft. The grass always grows back and I end up mowing it once a week.

My floors are wooden and linoleum. No rugs. Except for the kind that you can pick up, shake out and throw in the wash. I prefer my hardwood floors which have a protective coating. They sweep and mop up easily.

My car is a total dog car. It's a van. I have all my stuff in it that I mention in the chapter for What a Dog Walker's Car Should Have.

You need to be available for the business that comes your way. It would be great if everybody took their holidays all at the same times. If you could work for two weeks and then have two off wouldn't that be wonderful. Most people are able to make plans and stick to them. The reality is, my plans change all the time. Even when I get a couple of clients booked on the same dates, when one cancels, it changes everything. If I was scheduled to get that dog at a certain time and now that doesn't have to happen, it opens up a space in my schedule for something else. It could open up a whole extra day. Like the appointment I've been trying to make at the dentist is suddenly available. I could get my car tuned up now. I could get my hair cut because I haven't had time to cut it in about 6 months. Or just take a moment to shop for groceries or that piece of clothing I wanted.

I went through a time where I interviewed some people who answered my ad when I was looking for extra help with boarding. Some of the people I met and the houses that I saw were just not equipped for dogs at all. The people were nice enough but the house did not have the proper layout if you wanted to board a dog there. One woman told me that she didn't have a fenced yard but she can hook the dog's leash onto the clothes line and it can run back and forth. That was all I needed to hear from her. Another one, this man was doing renovations and I'm sure the place will look really nice once it is complete but his yard had all this scrap and junk in it and no place for a dog to play.

Another woman didn't tell me until the end of our interview that she would be working 9am to 5pm. These situations for boarding dogs just won't do.

I'm not saying that you have to put your life on hold in order to run a home boarding business but you sure do have to set your priorities in order. After all if you want to be successful then you will have to be accommodating. That means when the customer asks if you are available, then you BE available. You also really must be sincere about what you are promising. I have had people ask and be concerned if I will be home with the dogs or if I am out at night or out during the day. I work from home. So, yes I am here. I can say that because it is the truth. Holidays and weekends are the busiest times and that's where a lot of the sacrifices come in. I don't do many holidays with the family and so it doesn't bother me to work during those times.

I enjoy staying home, for the most part. I like to get out now and then but I do prefer to stay home and create a nice atmosphere. After all I am out all day with the dogs keeping them busy then the evenings are more my own. The dogs are tired from the long hard day of playing, so they sleep well at night. I like to find a soothing, relaxing feeling in the little things around the house. For some reason I am reassured when I am washing the dishes and I can see the reflection of the wood burning stove in the window. The warmth of the fire is comforting. Since this only happens in the winter, maybe that's why it's reassuring. I know that I am getting through yet another season.

The fall is my favorite time of year. It is so beautiful here when all the leaves have changed colors. It's just not long enough. This is the time of year when I like to do my spring cleaning.

Summer is probably my least favorite time of year. It's hot and it's usually a very busy time for boarding. Getting a day or two off is rather difficult but having extra help is a necessity for keeping my sanity. The administration part of this job takes a lot of keeping track. If I can manage to not talk to anyone for a half a weekend about my job, that can be quite a treat. Sometimes I really enjoy not even petting a dog for a day or two but y'know that is about as long as that feeling lasts. I like having a break now and then but I end up going through withdrawals after two days and I gotta pet a dog!

Rejection

A short note on the fact that a client may call you, interview you, even meet with you and then tell you that a "friend of the family" offered to take care of the dog for the week. Hmm…that friend of the family that was not available a few days ago when they were speaking with you but now all of a sudden the "friend" has had a change of heart.

Uh-huh. There's not much you can do about it even if you know that the person is lying to you. All you can do is be the bigger person and say thank you to them for letting you know and assure them that you will be there for them the next time they are in need of a boarding service. They might call you again. I have had people call me who I remember speaking to years ago. I'm not kidding. Sometimes certain things just stick in my mind and if the person said something particular to me that either upset me or just sounded funny and made me wonder, I might remember it and recall their name or the dog's name or just something about them. After years people have contacted me again and now they want to use MY service!

It is difficult when you have people come over to your house, look around while you explain to them what you do, then they go away and although it seems as if they were satisfied, they call you a few days later to tell you that they don't need to use your service. Or even worse you don't hear from them at all, you have to call them and be told that they meant to call to let you know that they don't need you.

It's hard to accept and there's nothing you can do about it. This business is very personal, so people will have many of their own reasons to not use your service and it may not be because of you or your house at all.

There was one woman who had two little dogs, and understandably she was worried about leaving them. I was trying to be very honest with her and well…sometimes being too honest can make people worry even more. I suppose I should not have explained to her in such detail how I was figuring the evening would go. Since she was worried that the dogs would miss her and might feel some separation anxiety when she left, I told her that I have been with dogs before that have taken a long time to settle down and sometimes it takes a day or two before they really start to adapt. I told her they might not want to eat their breakfast (they were dropped off at night) and I also expected that they might not sleep a whole lot this first night. She asked me what I would do if they didn't sleep. I said well, I guess I won't really sleep too much either. They can come up on the bed with me and I can try to comfort them and get them to settle down but I told her that tonight might be a long night for us. She could not fathom or believe me that I would be ok with this. I tried to tell her that I have done this before, it's not so bad. I tried to tell her that I could get the dogs to calm down and settle and that I'm sure we will all be fine. She told me how she would go crazy if she did not get any sleep at night. I tried to tell her that I have been through this sort of thing before and I did not mind doing whatever it is I had to do to get the dogs calm and relaxed and if it took a while before they settled it was fine with me. We were in Toronto at the time and were planning on going to the farm in two days. I told her once we get to the farm it will be a lot easier to deal with. Well, it seemed that the more I tried to convince her that it would all be ok and that I was fine with the situation and that I could actually handle it, the more she was talking herself out of leaving the dogs with me. She just didn't believe me. She was awfully neurotic and I wondered about her mental stability. She kept saying that she had a lot of pressure at her work and she had a big conference/presentation in two days and she could not be worrying about her dogs while she was away. I told her she doesn't have to be worrying. She just needs to trust me. Well, that just about did it. She started to get very anxious and started to pace in my living room, pulled out her cell phone and she said to her self out loud, "I need to make an executive decision!" I wasn't quite sure what was going on but I was beginning to take this personally and I told her so. I told her I think we have a personality clash and maybe if she had an alternative then she should use it. Then she said that she just wants her dogs to be taken care of. I said I could handle it. I realized now, that she did not believe me when I said that I would go out of my way to do whatever I had to do to make the dogs calm down and settle in.

I'm sure the dogs would have been fine after she left. Dogs can feel what you are feeling and they will feed off of you and react to the way you are feeling. So anyway, this woman decided to leave and took her dogs with her. I was truly offended and I told her that. She gathered up the dogs in a huff and was mumbling something. As she left, I told her that she has just created a lot more work for her self now and that was too bad for her.

Honestly, I know that I tried to work it out with her. We would have been fine. And I really would have gone that extra mile to care for those dogs. Some people know that of me. Others can believe what they want, the bottom line is, people keep coming back to me because they trust me. And nothing is more rewarding than getting that phone call from a past client that says they would like to leave their dogs with me again.

Keep in mind that you can say no to the client if you want. It is hard to learn to do that but you have to make some decisions for the sake of either convenience or safety.

I had one person keep asking me about my business insurance and what it covered.

It makes me nervous when the potential client asks me too many questions about something that I never plan on having to use. But granted I may have to someday, however, I can also make the decision to NOT take on any job that I think may be in some way detrimental to me or my dogs or my whole business. When a person asks me certain questions about how I handle possible situations, I tell them I have a backup plan. Then I ask them why they think I may end up in a situation. The best way to make sure that you will not have dog fights or injuries is to screen the dogs you plan to take in and make sure you walk the dogs in a safe place. Precautions must be taken as I said in The Face in the Window, prevention is key.

When I think that I may be entering a situation that could actually cost me more in the long run, I will not take that job. I'll simply make cut backs to my spending habits. Be aware of certain people that might not tell you the whole truth about their dog. If you think someone sounds like they may have other concerns, best to tell them that you think you may not be the right person to help them out. I would rather eat macaroni and cheese dinner for a week than have a person as a client that could risk damaging my whole reputation and life savings.

Information about different kinds of insurance can be found from the Professional Dog Walkers Association International website at www.prodogwalker.com

When a client that I hoped to have calls me and tells me that they decided to make other arrangements or use a friend, even though I am really disappointed and rather annoyed at the cancellation, I try to keep it pleasant. What's more difficult is when you can't get a callback to confirm if the client is booking with you or not. Sometimes you may call the client two or three times and have still not recieved a callback. On my thrid call to the client, I tell them that this will be the last call I make and I do not hear back I will assume that they are not booking with me. This for some reason usually gets the person to call me back right away.

The opposite could happen where the dog might not want to go home. I have brought back dogs that clearly did not want to go back to their home in the City.

This one dog Aggie a Springer Spaniel, turned and ran after me when I tried to leave the owner's house after bringing her back home. She darted towards the door as I went to leave. The owner loves the fact that her dog wants to go with me but at the same time I think she wonders who the dog prefers!

My dog, "Princess Kylie of the Tall Grass" at the end of our driveway.

Chapter 3

Feeding Time – Your Table is Ready

I mention later on as well that feeding your boarders on a set schedule is important; I also like to feed the dogs before I eat. I don't think it's fair that I sit down to my dinner when they are hungry. At least if I have fed them and they are full, then it is justified for me to tell them to back off if they try to get at my dinner!

I like to feed the dog's breakfast and dinner. On occasion I get a dog whose owner feeds their dog only once a day. Could be just breakfast or it could be just dinner. Feeding a dog once can be difficult to do if you have a larger number of dogs with you. If I only have two or three with me and I know what their eating habits are such as how they behave around food, then I can feed them without separating them with a gate. But usually and almost always, each dog has their own section for eating.

If two dogs are boarding with you that live together then maybe they can eat in the same area. I learned that the way the dogs eat has a significant impact on the decision of where to put them in my house when it is feeding time. Certain things such as whether a dog eats fast or slow, sloppy or neat or the sort of preparation the food needs. Perhaps it is a dog that eats a raw food diet or needs to have medication with the food. Even if I only have three dogs staying with me, I might have to block off everyone in their own sections due to one dog that throws his food all over the floor when eating; or another one that takes forever to chew and swallow; or another one that has to have a pill in the food. Each dog will have a different brand of food so making sure that they don't eat each other's food is important.

I separate them in their sections with baby gates. They all get used to the same area when I feed them in that spot every-day, twice a day. I can say to my dogs, "Ok, places everybody!" And the dogs will go to the spot where I have sent them before, and that's where they expect me to bring their dinner. The first time I might have to guide them into the area where I want them to be, then they realize, "this is the place where I get food", so they tend to go back there when I ask them.

You can find just about anything for dogs in the baby section of a store. As I already mentioned, I like to shop at second hand stores. Garage sales are also an excellent resource for dog supplies. Keep your eyes open, it's easy to make stuff out of other things as well. For example one of my gates to block off

Prepared meals for feeding time.

a doorway is the side of an old baby crib. It works perfectly since it has the vertical bars on the side which act as the barrier. Another one I have is a folding gate. I bought a couple of hinges from the hardware store and fastened it onto the wall. I pull the gate across the doorway or fold it flat against the wall when I'm not using it.

So, you must separate the dogs most of the time just for safety whether it is so they don't fight over the food or so they don't eat each other's food. There is a Golden Retriever that I board who must eat his dinner off of a plate. If he ate out of a bowl he would throw up. Of course putting his kibble on a plate made his feeding time very messy. It would fall off of the plate and spread all over the floor but he would still make sure he ate every piece of kibble. If any other dog was in the same area as him, he would not have the opportunity to finish all his food. Another dog would surely move in and eat it from him.

Then again, I have had dogs that eat at the same speed. So putting the food down on the floor with two dogs that eat fast, or even slow, as long it is the same speed, works ok. There was a black lab that would eat so fast that I was instructed to feed him a handful at a time and wait about a minute or so before giving him the next mouthful. It took about 8 minutes to feed this dog. He just ate too fast for him to handle it and would throw up due to his gulping it down.

One thing I always like to do especially with active dogs, is I take a cup of hot water and pour some of it in their bowl over their food and let it sit for a minute before I put it down for them. This makes the kibble expand so that when they eat it, they will digest it faster and easier. When kibble is eaten dry, it will expand in the dog's stomach and take longer to digest. Some dogs are really hyper and want to romp and play right after eating but I always wait at least 45 minutes before we go out for a walk after eating breakfast or dinner.

I should also mention that it is best to put the dogs securely in their dining areas before you prepare their food. If you have them all loose in the kitchen while you are putting the food in the bowls some of them could get a little too eager and excited which might entice a bit of a scuffle with the other dogs. I have had some really well behaved and patient dogs. It was so cute how they all sat and watched in amazement as I prepared their meals and poured the hot water over their food. They patiently waited while I struggled with the can opener! They drooled all over the floor but they waited until I said I was ready, then they all ran to their "places" and I put their food down for them.

I can't do that every time since I have different dogs here, but that particular group was unique.

After learning how early the dogs will wake me up for breakfast, I developed a trick. The more preparations I can do the night before to get the dog's breakfast ready for the morning, the better off I am in the morning to deal with frantic hungry dogs while I might still be stumbling half asleep. Tending to the dogs after you have been rudely awaken by 45 pounds of fur jumping on you, pawing at you, licking you or being woken by the sound of a piercing bark, is not too pleasant. The best thing I can do for myself in the mornings is to have all the dog's breakfasts already prepared in the bowls the night before. It is especially convenient to have food prepared when I have a larger number of dogs due to a holiday season. I put all the kibble in the bowls for each dog (all bowls are labelled accordingly) then I stack them on top of each other. I put a plastic bag over top of all the bowls to wrap it up nicely to keep it fresh overnight. When I get up in the morning, I take the bowls out from the cupboard, I spread them out on the counter, I get my measuring cup of hot water and I pour it over the food in each bowl. Breakfast is served.

After every meal, I always rinse out all the bowls under the tap and make sure there is no left over saliva or kibble bits. When the bowls are clean, I dry them with paper towel, check the labels to see if they are still secure and that I can read the dog's name and then I put the proper food in the proper bowls for each dog.

This of course is after I have let them out first thing to have their morning pee. Half asleep I usually throw on my coat and shoes and stagger out side to make sure they are behaving. When they come in, they eat and go out again after wards to do any more business they might need to do. The daily routine begins.

Lastly, I would just like to mention that sometimes a dog might not eat his dinner on the first day that he boards with you. He could be nervous. Chances are he will eat breakfast if he skips dinner, but if not, you could try a little parmesan cheese sprinkled over the food. I wouldn't try anything heavier than that unless the owner says it is ok. But always ask the owner if the dog is picky about his food, so that you know what you can and cannot try.

If a dog has diarrhoea then feeding him some white rice will help him to get back to normal. If he won't eat the rice on its own then mix it in with a bit of his kibble. No treats should be given until he is completely back to having solid poops.

Remember that fresh water is a part of their feeding time. I have two water bowls in the house and at least one outside. You might get a wise guy who likes to dump the water bowl or put his paw in it so be prepared to secure the bowl in some sort of heavy dish that cannot be tipped over. For a week I had to put my plastic water bowl inside a milk carton with a few bricks at the bottom so it was hard to tip yet still easy to access. That is just one of the many alterations and sacrifices you will be doing when you board dogs in your home. Now is a good time to ask yourself, what you are willing to change to make this work?

Personal feeding area.

Chapter 4

Real Overnight and Day Care

Sometimes having to get up in the middle of the night is part of the care that you give when you have other people's dogs in your home. It can be a tough call because if they come and wake you up, they could really need you or they might just be bugging you because they are lonely or bored or scared. But since they are right next to you, you could talk to them and try to calm them down. If they are really scared then you need to pay attention to that. I personally get up in the middle of the night and I will let them out if they are asking me to do that. However, do not give them any treats at that point — don't even pet them or talk to them a lot. If you give them any praise it will be seen as a reward for what they are doing and you will be training them to get you up at 2:00am in the morning every day. They know it's not yet 6am and not time for breakfast.

Occasionally you might find a little mess on the floor when you wake up if you haven't gotten up to let them out. But I would seriously consider the temperament and characteristics of the dog before you decide if you are going to get up in the middle of the night or not. You don't want to fall into a trap where they have a hold over you.

I had a very old, Old English Sheepdog named Jason that had to go pee but couldn't stand up on his own. He woke me up one night, I heard him kicking around on the floor and I got up out of bed to see what was going on. He was trying to stand up because he had to pee. I had to lift him up by his back legs with a towel holding him up underneath his stomach by his back legs so he could pee. I helped him up but he peed right there on the floor as soon as he stood up. I just had to grab the nearest towel and throw it down on the floor and let him pee on that. I cleaned it up afterwards. He took a few steps, got out of the puddle and then had to lie down again. What a sweet dog and I can't help think what if he were in a kennel and alone trying to stand up on his own, he wouldn't have made it and he would have peed all over himself and might have even hurt himself trying to stand up. I did not mind getting up in the night for Jason; after all, sheepdogs have a special place in my heart.

I want to mention when the dogs go home, how much of a sad feeling there can be when they do go home. An empty feeling. I brought a dog and a cat home after boarding with me for a week. They lived over top of a restaurant in downtown Toronto on a street that had four lanes of traffic. It's not my place to question it but I just felt so sad. The dog had been living with me on a 16 acre farm for a week and then he goes back to this apartment. I'm sure he was happy to see his owners and be home but I just felt so sad about it. Maybe I just liked this dog a lot. I have to wonder, because they really do have a great time on their stay here.

After a dog has been here for a week's stay, the clients all seem to say the same thing to me. When they get back home, the dog tends to sleep the whole next day. I believe the dog may be day dreaming about his experience here. When you come back from a nice vacation, don't you like to close your eyes and imagine you are back on the beach having fun? I think that is what the dogs are doing. They are reminiscing.

Ever wake up in the middle of the night to the sound of a dog puking? You will.

Ever wake up to the waft of fresh laid poop? You will. That's real pleasant; to get up out of bed in the middle of the night looking for the poop in your home because the smell of it woke you. You also hope that no one else has stepped in it in the meantime. I suppose that some other boarding places might think that this sort of thing is so easy to avoid because they keep the dogs in crates over night. When they are locked up they can't do these things to you and you don't have to get up in the middle of the night. Well, you know what? This is the way I prefer it. I like being in the same room as the dogs, on the same floor level as them and I like knowing exactly what is going on with them when it happens. I'd rather get up in the middle of the night and deal with something than find out about it the next morning. What if a dog puked or pooped or like Jason the Sheepdog, who couldn't get up on his own to pee, and I wasn't there to help? I can't imagine how any dog would feel going through that alone.

It is my choice to live this way. This is how I run my business. This is the kind of care I promise my clients and this is what they get.

I charge my boarding rate per day of boarding. I have some clients that barter with me and so depending on the situation I like to give discounts, but as a rule I don't have anything set in place such as weekly rates. I charge $35 a day at present. The days are what I charge by, not the nights. Some clients ask what I charge per night. Well, in that respect if I charged per night then they would be getting at least one or two days free.

If I had a dog coming over first thing Monday morning and leaving on Saturday night, if I charged by the night then a client might want to pay me for 5 nights which would be:

5 X 35 = \$175. What about all day Saturday? Or the first day, all day Monday? I worked and took care of the dog for the whole day. I see the time of boarding as being 6 days. Now I would give a discount of one day perhaps since the dog goes home on Saturday, if it was at a decent early hour. My days are 16 hours long and my nights are 8 hours, if I am lucky. So, yes I charge by the day. For the above scenario, I might ask for 5 days and one half day. I do charge a shuttle bus fee for a round trip sometimes, but it looks like I am giving a good discount if I say I will waive that fee. I give discounts all the time. The benefit of being a small business is that I can negotiate if I want to. I just like to keep it simple. It would depend on the dog itself and if he was a repeat customer or a new dog and how much trouble he might be to take care of. By that, I mean if he is trained, good off leash, needs any special attention, that sort of thing.

The other thing I have to take care of which is an ongoing task is all the scheduling that I arrange. I never know when someone is going to call me and book their dog in for a stay. So I don't always have exact times when I come into the City. It is always changing. It was suggested to me once that I pick certain days to drive in and set those days down as a regular schedule and then the clients would have to make the arrangements on the days that I am scheduled to come in. I thought this over and even tried it for a few customers and it did not work well for them to have to accommodate me, and I actually lost jobs.

So my idea of not having set days to have my "shuttle bus" works better. All I have to do is ask the customer when they are leaving and when they are coming back. I tell them up front that I may need for them to be a bit flexible because I may have to come into the City a day early to do the pick up which I would of course not charge them for the extra day. I also explain up front that I have an assistant who helps me out with short term and last minute boarding requests when I cannot be there to do it. I often use her house as the drop off and pick up location. When the client drops off the dog, I can usually be in to pick up the next day or later on that day. So I ask the client if they could be a bit flexible. I explain that if I had a dog that was starting to board on a Thursday, and another one that was to start on a Friday, I would ask the Friday dog client if I could pick up on the Thursday, a day early, and I would not charge the extra day. This saves me a trip into the City two days in a row. The same scheduling applies for the day that they go home. My assistant in the City can take a dog a day early and the client can pick up from her the next day. I use the same sort of method, a daily log schedule like the daily dog walks which I describe in chapter 13 of *The Face in the Window*. But you need to figure out a way to keep track which will work for you.

The client usually appreciates how much you do for them. A huge part of boarding dogs is about scheduling and making the arrangements. Then once you get to your destination for the next few days, you get to experience the thrill of living with all the different dogs and their personalities.

Now there will be a time when you have to leave your house and might not be able to take the dogs with you. I frequently have to do the drive into the City to pick up dogs and bring them home. Especially if it is hot out or if a dog does not travel well, I will leave them at home and have an assistant come in to walk them or to stay with them the whole time I am gone. I have met many kinds of people and have been disappointed many times with the people that I trusted. When I moved to the farm, I put an ad in the local paper to find some extra help. I met with a few people and there was one woman I liked very much. She really seemed to handle the dogs well. We made a deal that she was to stay at my house overnight with two dogs while I went into Toronto with some dogs and stayed overnight there. I was coming back the next day. The client's of the dogs were expected to come to the farm to pick up their dogs. That evening, the woman left my house and took the dogs back to her house. I only found this out when I called my home to check in with her and she did not answer. So I checked my phone messages and she had left me a message telling me that her dad was ill and she had to go home. I called her at her home and asked what had happened. She said her dad was ill and she needed to stay with him for the night. I asked where the dogs were and she told me that they were fine and they were in the garage. I did not know what I could have possibly done that evening so I just had to trust this woman that the dogs were ok. I asked her if the dogs were coming into her house for the evening and she said yes. I did not know if she was telling me the truth or not. But I knew at this point I would not be using her again. I told her that she had to get the dogs back to my house in the morning since the client's were coming to pick them up. Well, I got a call from the clients later that morning and they were furious with me. They told me that they got to my house and the dogs were not there. They waited for a bit and then this pick up truck drove up to the house with the client's two dogs in the back of the open truck! That was the first time I fired anyone. I explained to the client's that this was not the deal I had made with this person, and even though they told me that they understood and that they are glad that the dogs are ok, and things are fine, they never did call me ever again.

Another girl that was a recommendation from someone I did know and trust; she was the daughter of a woman who worked for a reputable groomer so I figured this was better. All I was asking of this girl was to stay in the house while I drove to Toronto and back in the same day. I used her twice only. A month later I discovered that she used my computer without permission and accepted picture files from an Internet message program. She also wracked up my phone bill with long distance calls.

Another girl that I started to use quite regularly, three or four times throughout the summer, all of the sudden was not around anymore. Like usual, we had a tentative agreement for the weekend, and I called to confirm. I was told by her dad that she went away for the rest of the summer. She did not give me any notice that she would not be available for the rest of the summer. She had left a very nice large glass bowl at my house on one of her overnights. So I kept it. And I'm not going to give it back!

I have been through quite a few people but have finally found some good help. You just need to keep on looking and go with your gut. I know it sounds cliché but even though you get references, it still doesn't confirm that they will be a good reliable, honest person.

Like I say throughout this entire book, it takes a certain kind of person to do this kind of job. You can't fake liking this job. I love living with dogs. I get such a kick out of the fact that they follow me around the house. They do this just because they might be nervous. I tend to think that they expect me to disappear through some trap door in another room if they don't follow me in there.

Never a Dull Moment

I've had quite a few run ins with local wildlife here in the country. I have some coyotes that tend to hold meetings once a month in my field in the middle of the night. Or maybe it's more like a convention. When I hear them, I can't tell how many there are or how close they might be. A few times I have seen one of them early in the morning running out of the field and into the woods. My dog has chased one away more than once. They usually are gone by the time the sun is up but sometimes we can see one of them hanging around. I learned later that my neighbour who has a corn field has one that comes around his place now and then to look for food. Even though it is tame it still runs away when it sees people and it sure runs away when it sees my dogs coming. I have never seen more than just the one hanging around in the field. I hope it stays that way. I have had a jack rabbit in the field that some of the dogs have chased out. But since I am always looking ahead in front of me at what's going on around me, the same way I did when walking dogs in the City, I see any obstacles and I can then prevent things from happening that I don't want. Often I spot the rabbit before the dogs and yell out to the dogs to "come this way", and I lead them in the opposite direction so the rabbit can run away. I've saved quite a few different kinds of wildlife here on the farm by looking out ahead.

Coming back from a walk I have to pass under a big tree to get into the gate to the yard. As I was getting the dogs into the yard, I heard this fluttering sound above me. I didn't think anything of it. A bit later on I had to get the garbage together and my bins are under that tree. As I was sorting the garbage, I heard the fluttering again. I looked up this time and even though I could hear the flutter, I could not see anything. Until I looked closer. I could see a tiny little bird flapping his wings and kicking his feet but not moving. He had himself stuck in the branches of the pine tree. But the reason why he was stuck was because his foot was wrapped with some stuffing material that came out of a stuffed animal that the dogs had ripped apart and spread all over the ground. I felt awful. I know he wanted the stuffing for his nest but that was why he got stuck. I got my ladder and climbed up to get a closer look at him. I had to go back in the house and grab a pair of scissors; I would have to cut him free. The stuffing was wrapped around his little foot and I was able to cut it from the side of his leg. He flew away the moment I got his leg free. I took away the excess stuffing and brushed the dogs outside so the brids could use the dog fur instead.

But I have had to kill or dispose of already dead things too. That is the downside of living here. It was pretty awful one day that I had to kill a frog that I accidentally ran over with the riding lawnmower. I saw him on the ground after the grass was cut shorter and he was on his side trying to keep hopping. When I looked at him closer I could see that I had run over him and he was cut pretty bad. There was no way I could help him...except to kill him. When you know something is suffering so bad that putting it out of its misery is the best thing to do, you would be amazed at what you can do. I ended up just hitting him with a brick a few times. I did not enjoy it at all and I screamed as I did it, but I knew that I had to do something. It would have been worse to leave him the way he was.

Another bad thing happened with another frog. This time I had been away from the farm for a few days in the summer and when I got back I was cleaning up around the yard and went to pick up a bucket to get some water for the dogs. When I looked in the bottom of the bucket, I noticed that there was a tiny frog in it. But he was not moving. He was dried up. He had been stuck in the bottom of the bucket and not able to get out. It rushed through my mind what must have happened, and what he must have gone through, being stuck there like that. I was devastated and I cried about it. It was my fault for not leaving the bucket on its side when I was not using it. Now when I go anywhere for days or just when any bucket that I have is not in use, I make sure I leave it on its side. I'm not joking; it is a priority of mine now.

On a lighter note, I had just arrived home from the City and was still unpacking the car. The few dogs I had with me were good off leash and so I let them hang around outside the yard on the circular driveway while I went in and out of the house with all their stuff. Just as I walked out of the door to head back to the car, my dog started to bark ferociously towards the opening of the driveway. Then of course all the others followed suit and started barking. My dog started to run down the driveway. So with all this happening in a matter of seconds, I ran towards the ruckus and what I saw was my dog chasing a cow down the driveway onto the dirt road. The other dogs did not go as far as Kylie did but they put up a tough front. I had just got back from the City, and this was the first thing to happen. My dog stopped at the end of the driveway at the dirt road and the cow was now being wrangled by a farmer on a tractor.

One time a dog that I had here that I should have had on leash went missing. It was time to get in the car and start looking around. As I drove up my road I did not see anything, so I turned around and drove the other way along the road. I hadn't noticed that the horses were out in the field next to me until all of a sudden I hear one of the horses make their "neighing" horse sound. It was loud and it got my attention so I stopped the car and stuck my head out the window and yelled out, "so do you know which way he went?" The horse did not make another sound, but he turned his head from looking at me to facing the direction of my house. I called out to him again, "hey, over here, have you seen my dog?" The horse did not move his head or make a sound. I then had a thought. Was this horse trying to tell me something? His head movement was so sharp and he froze facing that direction. I decided to drive back up to my place. To my amazement, as I drove up the driveway, I saw Snoopy trotting along happily coming out from the bushes. Did that horse tell me where the dog was? I don't know, what do you think?

I want to mention quickly, a little thing I do when I am driving in my car. If I see any critters at the side of the road, I always honk my car horn many times to try to scare them off the road. I've avoided hitting cats many times by doing that.

Since my neighbours are horses and cows, sometimes the neighbours get nosey and want to get a closer look at the dogs. The dogs can get curious too; I learned (the hard way) that I had an opening in the fence. A Lab X named Benny got through the fence and chased the cows. It was not funny at the time but I can laugh about it now. What happened was all of a sudden I saw all these cows running in one direction. Then I realized they were being rounded up by Benny. He was not coming as I was calling him. So I had to go into the field and try to get him. He was impossible to catch. If I got close to him he would slip out of my reach and run off towards the cows again. This went on for about 15 minutes and I was getting really tired of running after him and calling him. He was getting way too close to the cows and I was afraid he was going to get hurt. The cows would run away from him when he charged at them but then some of them would run towards him when he got a bit distant. When I finally got a hold of him, I grabbed his collar and locked my hand around it. He was tired too so he didn't fight with me when I walked him back to my place. However the problem now was, since I had a hold of him the cows figured this was their big chance for revenge. All the cows started to run towards me as I walked him across the field. These cows were serious, they wanted pay back. I've never been so close to cows before. In fact I had to push one cow's head away from me with my hand as I yelled at him to get away from us. I had no idea what the cows could be capable of. It was as I said, not funny at the time!

Once you are tuned in to knowing the different sounds that dogs make when playing, and how the sounds can mean different ways of communicating within the pack, then you can figure out when something is wrong just by hearing the sound of the bark. The group of dogs, I had were heading out on our walk up to the field, then I heard some frantic barking sounds coming from under the pine trees. I ran up to it because it just didn't sound right. Sure enough, three dogs had this porcupine surrounded and they were all barking at it! Well, I screamed at the top of my lungs for everyone to leave it alone and come this way. When my voice reaches a certain octave, mostly everything will listen to me. I got the dogs away from the porcupine and into the yard, closed the gate and went back to see if he was still there. Yup, he was. Porcupines do not move very fast. I thought what do I do, what do I do? I can't leave him there. I can't have him on my property anywhere! Since he wasn't running away I had some time to think. I came up with the master plan. I grabbed the big dog crate and carried it up the stairs from the basement and outside to the porcupine. I put it on the ground and said, "Ok, get in." No, he wasn't going to comply.

Since he wouldn't get in the crate I had to come up with a way to trap him. Good thing that porcupines don't move very fast. But when I moved he moved. I ended up picking up the crate and holding it over my head and when I started towards him, he started to scurry away from me (as fast as porcupines can scurry). So I actually chased him for a few feet holding this crate above my head before I was able to plonk the crate down over top of him and trap him inside. Now it was just a matter of getting the door closed and locked, getting the crate with porcupine into the car and driving out of the area!

Once he was trapped in it he was very cooperative. Other than when I had to move the crate by tipping it sideways to let the door swing in the proper direction to close it, I almost lost him when he tried to sneak out of the opening. I talked to him the whole time I was getting him prepared and letting him know that I as wasn't trying to hurt. I kept telling him I was going to take him to some nice other pine trees. The crate was heavy with him in it and since it had no metal bottom the poor guy didn't have anything to stand on except the bars. I was having a hard time moving the crate and did not know how I would get it in the car. I drove the car over to him so I didn't have to drag the crate across the ground. I needed to drag the crate across just a bit to get him up to the car and I noticed that his little feet were getting pinched when I moved the crate. But then I saw that this porcupine was pretty smart because every time I moved the crate, he would move his feet and stand on the bars so that he was riding on the bars instead of getting his feet caught between them. He was also holding onto the bars of the crate with his paws.

I slid the crate up into the car with a ramp that I use for old dogs that have a hard time geting into my car. And voila! The porcupine was ready to be relocated.

I think he was appreciative. I let him out in another forested area so I'm sure he is doing just fine. I'm just glad that I found him without any incidents with the dogs. I was happy that I didn't get hurt either. If you ever find your self confronted with a porcupine...umm...don't pet him!

Porcupine incarcerated!

I let sleeping puppies lie!

Roxanne enjoying some evening television.

Chapter 5

Itinerary for Day and Nighttime

Well, you're going to be woken up pretty early and there is no ignoring a bunch of hungry dogs first thing in the morning. They will lick you, breathe on you, and possibly jump on you. I stumble out of bed at 6am and let them out. I throw on my jacket and shoes and stand outside with my poop bag in hand barely awake, waiting for dogs to poop so I can pick it up. Once that is done we go inside for breakfast. They get to eat; I don't get to eat just yet.

It is important for dogs to stay on a set schedule and have activities during the day so they don't get bored. A bored dog can lead to many things such as being destructive or even aggressive. A typical day begins with breakfast, then after they have eaten and been let back outside, depending on the kind of dogs I have with me, if I am lucky I can maybe go back to sleep for another hour or so. Then, due to the dogs insisting that I have slept long enough, I stumble once again out the door for our first walk of the day. This is at about 7:30 or 8am. When we have done our first once around the field, I am very much awake now and ready to have my tea and some breakfast.

When a dog can be off leash and it plays well with other dogs, then they are going to have an amazing time. I like to take the dogs out about every two hours throughout the day. I find that after we go out for a half hour to 45 minute romp, they settle down nicely for about two hours before they start to rustle around and get playful again.

You have to be the one in charge. The dogs will listen to you as long as you know how to communicate with them. It may seem that you have given in but really you are just adapting so the dog can understand you. I have a story for you about a dog on my bed. I don't usually board male dogs that are not neutered but this one had been at my house before with its owner who dog sat for me and stayed over at my house a few times. I was careful to only have a small group of dogs of either females or very good dogs that did not have issues with another male dog not neutered when they came over. She needed my help at one point and I ended up boarding her dog, his name was Toby. Toby was the kind of dog that would jump up on you very gently as if to give you a hug. This, the owner thought, was really cute. I put up with it for the time being. I knew that this was the dog's way of saying "I can dominate you." Toby was a bit pushy and demanding when he wanted attention. So I would ignore him at times and pet him when he didn't ask for it. But at one point he jumped up on my bed and I did not want him up there. I told him to get off my bed and he growled at me. He refused to move. I was surprised and shocked and a little scared at first too. In my initial reaction I said, "Excuse me? What the hell do you think you are doing?" Then I told him firmly to get off my bed. He lay down on my bed and growled at me again. I was about to try the firm talk again but didn't because when I exhibited that attitude, his growl escalated and he wasn't about to stop. I did not want to get into a power war with him. I stepped back and looked at him with a look as if to say, "You are such a silly dog!" Then I started to talk to him in a normal tone of voice.

I said, "Toby, I don't like you very much. I can't wait for your owner to come back and take you away. I'm really looking forward to you leaving. Yes I am! I can't wait." Toby was now listening to me and looking at me attentively. I then sang him a little song: "Goodbye Toby, farewell you Poo…if I ever see you again, it'll be too soon." At this point he was now sitting up on the bed and his mouth open and relaxed with tail wagging. He had no idea what I was saying to him but the tone of my voice was easing him. He was not being aggressive, he was listening to me. I then said, "Hey Toby c'mon this way", and I ran out of my room and he jumped off my bed following me out. I put a gate across the doorway to prevent that from happening again! I then just ignored him most of the time that he was with me until he went home.

Eye contact and petting a dog can establish that you are dominant over the dog. However, when you have a dog that wants the attention at his beck and call…then it is better that you give him the opposite behaviour.

Daily Clean Up

Sometimes you might have a client that calls and wants to come over last minute. Maybe it is a new client coming to see you, so you will want to make a good impression.

I don't like people thinking that they can pop by unannounced. I'm not a storefront. It's my home. People must first call and give me at least a half an hours notice.

Sometimes you have to do what I call a "frantic rush of cleaning up."

This is when I just have to straighten things up to make the place look tidy and presentable. I clear off the counters and do the dishes and straighten the covers on the sofa and chairs. If I have time I'll sweep the floor. For a quick clean up I have used those dust cloths that you attach to the rubber mop, and run it across the floor. This will pick up most of the loose hair and clumps of dust when I have not had time to stay on top of cleaning. If you use those dust cloths everyday, you will find that the amount of dog hair that accumulates is minimal but if you skip a day, you can see how much dog hair can collect. I have flooring all over the house and only use those rugs with the rubber backs that I can throw in the wash. But if your house has rugs, you will need a really powerful vacuum and you should be vacuuming once a day.

One important thing you have to not ever forget about is to clean yourself up. No matter what your place looks like, you can explain that you didn't have time to put away your laundry or whichever but how do you explain that you didn't have time to wash your face or brush your hair or brush your teeth! I like to wear sweatpants and so I usually have them on all the time, except for when someone comes over. Then I put on jeans or something that doesn't look so frumpy. It is so important that you look presentable. Put your hair in a ponytail or put on a hat, if brushing it isn't enough. Get out of your dog clothes and put on something a bit nicer. The way you look makes just as good or as bad an impression as the way your house looks.

Smells are another thing. When I'm in a pinch, I will spray around those fabric refreshers. I don't use them regularly. I will otherwise just do a lot of laundry which is a big part of my daily itinerary.

I like to have all the covers and blankets as clean as they can get and to always be that way. So I am doing about one load of laundry a day. And I like to use strong fresh smelling detergent with fabric softeners and bleach when needed. Due to my layers of sheets covering my furniture, I can take off the top layer and have an instant clean cover.

During my frantic rush of cleaning up, a quick thing you can do for smells is to take a fabric softener sheet and rub it all over your couch and other furniture. Then throw it in the garbage can so the garbage smells nice too. I place fabric softener sheets in the bottom of my garbage cans and in my closets as well. But make sure you wash your hands afterwards because when you go to shake the hand of the client coming over, you don't want to overwhelm them with your fresh smells. Another quick fix for smells, is to spray some bathroom cleaner, the kind used to clean the bathtub or tiles. Spray that in the bathtub and rinse some water around in it and you will have a fresh smelling bathroom. Just don't over do it because that smell can be very strong and carry all throughout the house.

I keep a few of those scented oil air fresheners that plug into the wall, on hand. I will plug them in when I have someone coming over, and then I take them out after they leave. I don't like to have them plugged in all the time. I find the smell can be a bit overwhelming and I think of how the dog's nose is so much more sensitive than ours.

So I only put them in one or two rooms at a time. Sometimes just making sure your garbage is out and your sink is clean can be enough to keep the smells down.

If you smoke, which I don't recommend you do if you are going to consider boarding dogs in your home, that will be another smell that you will have to eliminate. I don't smoke but have known others that do. What I learned from them is lighting some candles in the house when a cigarette is lit will help to get rid of the smoke in the air.

As I said, I don't recommend it but if you do smoke, please be considerate of the space that the pets are in. This also applies for when you are driving in the car. For the most part smoke outside.

When it rains, things get messier. I usually have a whole bunch of blankets and towels stored away and ready to set down to replace the dirty blankets. I go through more clean towels and blankets on rainy days than any other day. Since I want to keep on top of it, I do more laundry so I don't end up short of clean blankets for the dog beds. I replace the dog beds at least once a week or every few days depending on the weather and the condition of the dog. Some dogs shed more than others but are clean and dry so what I do is pick up all the blankets that I have on the floor for the dogs, bring them outside and shake the blankets furiously to get all the fur off them. You will notice that certain kinds of material repel fur better than others. Never use a wool blanket for a dog.

Cotton is really the best. Most of the time fur shakes off of that easily. Another quick trick to get fur off of your covers is to throw it in the dryer for 10 minutes. To get fur off of your furniture, wear a pair of rubber gloves and dip them in a bowl

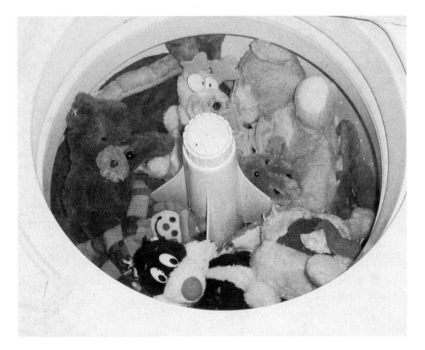

Washing the toys for the dogs!

of water and while damp, run your hands over the couch or chair and the fur will all pile up into a big ball. Keep doing that until you get it all off.

A daily shaking out of the blankets, the beds, the covers and the rubber backed rugs will keep things fairly neat. There will be fur when you live with dogs, so get used to it. Just keep on top of it. My place is cleaner and tidier than some people's houses who only own one dog. Then again, I am here all the time, like a stay at home mom, so I can clean more often. I constantly have something to do, be it laundry, or sweeping, washing dishes, sorting dog food, dusting, returning emails or phone calls, all my daily administration for my business as well as for the Professional Dog Walkers Association, writing articles for pet magazines or working on my other writing projects or all the stuff I have to do outside of the house to keep the farm looking neat and tidy. I have to mow the lawn in the summer and shovel snow in winter and there's a lot more room to clear around this house than a house in the City.

In between all that I walk the dogs about every two hours. Oh yes, and I have to eat now and then too. So there certainly is never a dull moment with all the things that can go on in and around the farm.

Out On The Walks
While out on a walk take note of where the dog sniffs on the ground. You always have to watch which directions they are heading off to so you can look out for what is on the ground. If they are sniffing the ground then get to that spot and have a look at what is there because there is a reason why the dog stopped. See what is there, pick it up and take it away. Get rid of it, otherwise they will go back there again and again. Much of the same advice given earlier in *The Face in the Window* on walking dogs is applicable here. I would advise that the num-

ber of dogs that you walk would be the best way to determine how many dogs you should board. The industry standard is 6 dogs for walking. So depending on where you live, boarding should also reflect the industry standard. Although some juris-dictions would only allow you to board 3 dogs which reflects the laws on the number of dogs allowed owned in a household. Regardless, do not take on more than you could handle out on a daily walk. Remember that with daily dog walking you can put them back at their home, but the dogs you are boarding, have to come back to your house — be careful who you take in.

When I have a first time boarder with me and I don't know for sure how they are off leash, I always put that dog on a long rope for the first walk. I have 3 long ropes that are of different lengths and weight. The longest is the heavier, thicker rope about 20 feet. The other 2 are shorter and lighter. They all have a good solid clip on the end. A new dog that I'm not so sure about will go on the long heavy rope. I'll hold onto it and see how they react when I call them. If they are attentive, I will drop the rope on the ground.

I'll be paying close attention to them and watching them to see if they are going to bolt off ahead. If they do, I would have to run at least 20 feet behind them to catch up and step on the rope to get a hold of them.

I've had to use all three ropes on dogs here before. I have to be careful with them until we get up the field then I can drop the ropes and let the dogs drag it. I make sure that they don't get tangled. Eventually, the dogs will graduate to not needing the rope at all.

When they are off leash what I find is, the dogs tend to want to play with each other more than anything and so they end up following each other. The ones that listen to me, follow me and the others follow those dogs. I know that every dog is different. I make sure that I make a bond with each dog individually.

If you are able to walk your boarders on your own property then you will have an easier time of getting through the days that are either really hot or really cold. It is summer time right now and we are in the middle of a heat wave. The dogs get me up at 6am and our first walk might be at 7am. I take them out about three times before 11am. We have to stay inside with the air conditioning until later in the afternoon before we venture out again. Quick outings might be ok since you are home with the dogs, and they will have your company in the house, therefore spending the day inside is not so boring for them. It is the safest thing to do.

No matter where you live a dog can always find something smelly to role in. In my case I have had a few dogs find cow pies and roll over top of them. Then it is bath time! I leash them to go back to the house and into the bathroom shouting in my best Planet of the Apes impression, "Get your paws off me you damn dirty dog!"

I should mention that the woman who did the cover of this book, Catherine Gillespie, told me about a fun summer treat for dogs that I would like to share. She makes beef bullion ice cubes for her dog! I thought what a yummy and refreshing treat on a hot day!

My boarding assistant Bev, showed me how she uses some old socks to wipe off the dog's paws before they come inside. Just stick your hand into the sock and it makes it easy to get right in between the pads.

I purchase flea/tick collars every few months to have on hand for all my boarders. I do ask for each dog to be on a flea prevention treatment but you can also purchase certain treatments at pet stores, however ask the owner first if they want you to do that. I have flea premise spray on hand and dog and cat shampoo as well. I'll mention that the best remedy I have used for a light spray of skunk which occurred with a dog, was the use of toothpaste lather. I rubbed toothpaste on the spot where the dog was sprayed and added water to make it lather. It worked wonders and took away the smell instantly.

My own dog knows that when I tell her to be "careful" it means that she should be aware that she could get hurt. I say that word whenever there is the possibility of danger nearby. I also say it when she does get hurt. That way when I say it before something has happened, she hears it as a warning that she could get hurt.

While At Home
You don't want to watch certain T.V. shows when you have a group of dogs living at your home. Wheel of Fortune is not a great show to watch. I'll tell ya, when someone gets a letter correct and all those "dings" go off…you could have a bunch of dogs exploding into barking fits. I had a dog that charged the television set every time a certain commercial came on that had another dog running in it. Dogs can definitely see the T.V. and they know when an animal sound is coming from it. If you ever did leave the dogs alone, what I like to do is leave on the radio or the T.V. Just don't leave the T.V on a channel that has wild animals on it all the time.

I have to tell you about a dog named Hershey and how I discovered that he could not be left alone ever — unless I park a car in front of the fridge! I went out to an exercise class, was gone for only 2 hours and when I came back, my kitchen looked like it had been ransacked! The refrigerator was wide open and so was the top freezer part of it. Not sure how he got up high enough to open the freezer but I had empty frozen food wrappers all over the floor and most of the contents of the fridge spread out all over the floor as well.

When I picked everything off the floor and identified it, I wrote down everything that he ate:

3/4 of a pumpkin pie, frozen French fries and corn dog TV dinner, English muffins, a frozen chicken breast, and some frozen chicken strips. What he didn't eat in the fridge was an opened can of dog food and a bowl of left over kibble from breakfast. He didn't take anything off the counter either. He just went straight for the fridge and freezer.

Fights and Bites
You want to have all the same stuff in your home that you have in your pet first aid kit in your car as well as some other things on hand. An antihistamine such as some Benadryl™ is good to have. This is something that veterinarians in my past experience have given to dogs after a bee sting. I had a dog whose face puffed up. I did not see if it was a bee sting. I rushed him to the vet and they gave him an injection of Benadryl™. The swelling went down in a few hours. I thought afterwards that I could have done that at home. I bought some and now keep it available. It comes in liquid and pills. I have used it once before on a dog when some little hives appeared on him. I squirted some of the liquid in his mouth with a syringe and the bumps were gone in an hour. Dogs will get into things and may have an allergic reaction. It is important to know when to take a dog to the vet and when to know that you can treat him at home. This is why taking a Pet First Aid Course is so important! You should not panic if something happens. But you also have to know when it is time to take a dog to the vet. I recommend calling up the dog's vet and telling them what the situation is and that you have some supplies and ask for advice on whether you should administer anything. Boarding dogs is a huge responsibility and it should not be taken lightly. You'll need to get a list of vets in your area and make sure that you have one that offers 24 hour emergency service.

If the dogs have been in a scuffle and you don't see any visible marks or cuts right away, then start checking the areas that were targeted at the time of the scuffle. Most scuffles might occur around the heads of the dogs so check thoroughly the ears, the lips and all around the mouth and the eyes. Look at the fur around the neck. Dogs can grab each other's necks and may end up ripping a bit of skin that you might not see right away. If you find one small puncture wound, keep checking that area for another small puncture. There are usually 2 marks when there has been a bite; one from the upper jaw and one from the lower jaw.

Run your hands all over their body checking for cuts. Keep an eye on the dogs breathing, its appetite and its general nature. Reading a dog and identifying if there is a problem comes with time and experience. This is why I suggest that if you want to do dog boarding as a full time job, you ought to have the daily dog walking experience behind you first.

It will not always be rosy, happy, perfect days with perfect dogs all the time. For whatever reasons dogs can turn and start to fight with each other. It may be a quick scuffle over who owns the stick on the ground or it might be a fight that can last longer than you expected. So you need to know beforehand when you have to be particularly careful with a dog. I feel I caused a fight one time when I through a ball for a dog and didn't notice that another dog nearby went for the ball at the same time. When the dog I intended to catch the ball met with the other one, a fight ensued and bites were inflicted.

If I had paid better attention I could have prevented that situation. Something you could do which I realized afterwards, is always throw one ball in one direction and another ball in another direction to prevent these crashes. I had to take that dog to the vet. There were too many bite marks and one of them was rather large.

What happened was, the top layer of the skin was ripped open but luckily there were no major punctures. The vet did not want to stitch the dog but rather put him on antibiotics and gave me a topical solution to treat the wounds. When I told the owner, she was very understanding. She understood and told me that her dog was a bit possessive when it came to chasing balls and she said she forgot to tell me that. I told her I did not want any money from her for the boarding. She paid me back for the vet bill. But she insisted on paying me for the boarding too. So I told her to only pay me half. She still paid me the full price and at that point I burst into tears in front of her. She gave me a hug and told me not to worry about it, handed me the money and then reached for a beer from out of the cooler in her trunk. She said I looked like I could use it. She was an extraordinarily, exceptionally nice person.

A bit of daytime activity.

Chapter 6

Out, Standing in My Field

If you get to a point in your business when you are happy that someone has cancelled their booking with you, then you are probably doing very well. I have been happy once or twice from a cancellation. But then you do have these dry spells where there is no business for you for weeks or maybe you only have one or two dogs to board at a time.

Try to enjoy it I say. When you don't have a lot of work to do, why not use the time to put your house and business in order? Learn a new computer program or clean out a filing cabinet. This spring for the first time I was able to try some gardening.

It was fun, and new for me since I was busy last year at this time, I completely missed out on all the opportunities to try gardening. In fact I missed out on noticing all the kinds of flowers that bloom in the spring. For the first time I stopped to smell the flowers.

I try to remember things like this now, and as I walk through my field, I like to reflect on what I have accomplished. We have all accomplished something and we can all do much more. If you plan to start your own business, you will have a great feeling of independence and you should know that you can make it work. My advice is to not get too far into it until you are comfortable. I believe you should start by walking dogs and then ease yourself into boarding.

When you have down time use it for something that you don't get to do when you are working so hard. Concentrate on your business, think of some new marketing ideas. After all, marketing is much about taking the idea that someone else has done and making it your own.

I have seen a lot of my own ideas and written material out there with someone else's name on it. Even though I may not have been the only one to have come up with certain things, I do know for a fact that some ideas have been my own. Imitation is supposed to be a form of flattery but when it comes down to how hard you have worked at something and then someone else taking credit for it, I will not stand for that and neither should you. Once you have built up your business make sure that you confront anyone who might copy your material from your website and your logos as well.

Here's a little acronym that you can use when you talk to clients or employees. I call it C.A.R.E. I try to keep this in mind when I need to communicate effectively. This is what it stands for:

C- Compliment and Credit
A- Assert and Accommodate
R- Reiterate
E- Encourage (the outcome you want)

Feel good about doing your job and doing it well. Try not to worry too much about competition. I am not a huge business at all. I just get by for myself, and am trying to stay happy with what I do. You will never be able to please everyone. I'm very careful with my money as we all should be. It makes a big difference when you know that saving money is not about how much money you make but how much money you spend. There are many ways to make your dollar stretch. It is true that you have to spend some money to make money, but you can find other ways to promote your business that don't have to cost you an arm and a leg.

One bit of advice when you are reporting back to the client about how their dog was during its stay with you. If you didn't enjoy everything about the dog, try to not make it sound like it was all bad. You need to make light of it unless there is a really serious issue with the dog. If you complain in any way about the dog, that client will never call on you again. So if you do have to say something negative, make sure you give a suggestion on how the dog could do better or tell the client how you dealt with it and what worked for you. Basically, don't just say your dog was unruly, obviously you had to get through the time that he stayed with you so tell them what you did. They might appreciate the advice. With the right client who has the right sense of humour, I like to tell them how wonderful their dog was during the time he was with me, especially how good the dog was when he was sleeping.

Here is some information which I tell my clients when they inquire about Sleepover Boarding. This info is on my website as well and may have been updated since.

- *Sleepovers consist of day and overnight supervision in a home environment rather than a typical "kennel" style.*
- *Your dog must be* **well socialized** *and* **friendly** *with other people and pets. Your pet needs to be up to date on his/her shots.*
- *First time boarders are given a slower integration into the pack and have extra supervision until a comfortable stance is established.*
- *It is preferred that your dog be on a flea control program. If you would like your dog to be placed on a flea control program during the course of the boarding period, we can do so for a fee of $10.*

The flea control will last for up to one month.

- *Our boarding facility is located in a country setting just outside the town ofLindsay.*

Please have a look at the Photo Gallery.

WE CAN COME TO YOU - *A door to door shuttle bus is provided to certain areas, when it is applicable. A round trip fee of $15 and one-way trip of $10 applies. Drop off and pick up locations inToronto can be arranged.*

*Our guests always enjoy at least, **three walks a day** on the 16-acre field with groomed trails, hills and a fenced yard in which to relax. We venture out every few hours throughout the day to walk through the entire field which is usually four to eight walks a day. The walk time is the length of about 25 to 45 minutes. My "camp" groups are small. On average there are six dogs at a time as I like to keep the care and supervision on a personal, intimate level.*

Nighttime is spent indoors in the lounge area where our dog guests choose a quilt to curl up on or sleep on their own bed that you provide.

Feeding time is according to the schedule that you provide. Otherwise we eat breakfast and dinner. The dogs wake me up at 6am and dinner is usually served at 6pm.

YOU MUST SUPPLY YOUR DOG'S OWN FOOD PLEASE. Check in and Check out times may vary and half-day rates may apply.

A Toll Free number for your convenience is available to call and check up on your pet.

Digital Postcards of your dog at play during their stay are provided via e mail.

Here is a sample of an application form if you plan to hire others for boarding:

Established Dog Boarding facility looking for reliable trustworthy caring individuals to board pet dogs in your home temporarily. Earn money in exchange for companionship and fun! Call for an application. 1-800-275-0910 or email dianne@jogadog.ca

APPLICATION FORM FOR
JOG-A-DOG PET SERVICES

Boarding a dog in your home is much like fostering a dog that is looking for a new home. However the length of time that a boarder stays is limited and the owner of the dog(s) will be coming back. You will be responsible for feeding, walking, and keeping your boarder safe until the end of their stay with you.

Name: _____

Address: _____

Phone numbers: _____

Do you drive? _____ Do you have your own car? _____

Driver's license number: _____

Please list 2 past occupations with start and finish dates.

_____

_____

Have you ever worked with animals in the past?

_____

Have you ever worked with a pet care professional, such as a dog trainer, groomer, kennel, or Veterinarian? Taken any agility or obedience classes? Please list experience:

_____

_____

Do you have pets of your own?

_____

Where do your pets sleep?

_____

Is your pet, Male, Female, Spayed, Neutered? (*Please circle/state appropriate term*)

Do you have any dependants? _____

Do you smoke? Yes   No   Socially.
(*Please circle/state appropriate answer*)

Are you available to come and sleep over at the boarding facility?

_____

Would you be interested in boarding a cat at your home?

_____

Boarding a dog is a very personal experience. Caring for someone else's pet needs to be taken seriously and it must blend into and suit your lifestyle. Please answer these questions honestly in order to make the right decision for everyone. In return you will make some extra money, develop a daily exercise routine and enjoy the companionship of a pet dog.

- *If you have pets of your own, will they be friendly with other dogs?*
- *If you have cats, would you put them in a separate room?*

- *Do you have antique rugs?*
- *Do you have valuables that are low to the ground or somewhere that could be easily knocked over?*
- *Do you understand what puppy/dog proofing is?*
- *Is your yard completely fenced?*
- *Where will you walk the dogs?*
- *Where will the dogs sleep?*
- *Are you willing to get up and let the dogs out when they show they need to pee or poop? (It could be odd hours of the night)*
- *Are you comfortable with giving a dog medication, such as pills?*
- *Do you often have to go out and leave the house during the day and/or the evening?*
- *Do you have an area to confine the dog(s) if they must be left alone?*
- *Do you have an area in which you could put a crate?*
- *Do you have gates to section off rooms of the house for feeding times?*
- *Do you often have guests over?*
- *Would you ever have children over at your house?*
- *Would your guests be dog friendly with a common sense approach to meeting a dog?*
- *Do you have any health problems or concerns?*

You want to know typically what the person is going to be doing all day and what they plan to do with the dog all day. You have to be just as careful with hiring as you would be with daily dog walking. It's the same personal touch that you are looking for. And I know it's a cliché, but good help is hard to find.

Just playing...really!

Some Boarding Reference Letters:

Thanks for the great pix. Meggie was happy to be home of course and must have gotten a lot of exercise with her new buddies, because she climbed onto my bed at 7 p.m. and went right to sleep! She never got up again until this morning at 7 a.m.She sure looks like she was enjoying her "sleepovers". Thanks again Dianne for the great care! We'll see you soon — when I know exact dates for my upcoming conferences.

K. Park

Thank you Dianne. Roxy LOVED going to Jog-a-Dog! She always had a blast and when she got home she slept for three days straight! Thank you for always taking such good care of her and making her feel so loved. That picture is an absolute howl — we love it and I am glad to know it's on your web site — we'll take a browse through it again. We will always recommend your service to other dog lovers and if we get

another fur-child, we'll be sure to call on your warm and caring company.

All the best Dianne. Sincerely, Sharon
ROXANNE - OCTOBER 24, 1997–JUNE 23, 2005.

Hi Dianne,

Just a short note to say thank you for taking such good care
of Murphy. She got in the car and would not look at us until
the next day. We figure she missed you. However, she is back
to her old self and we are happy we found you.

We are contemplating a trip to Chicago sometime during the last two weeks of Sept. I will give you lots of notice.

Thanks again.
John and Michel

Lastly, I want to leave you with the thought that if you do
really want to board dogs in your home, much of the same rules
apply for when you are dog walking. Your work will never be
done. But working for yourself and running your own business
is supposed to be about enjoying yourself and your job.

The way I see it is, money you can always make back, but
time you can never get back. It doesn't cost me anything when
I look out my kitchen window to the neighbour's field where I
appreciate seeing the family of horses grazing. I watch the tops
of the trees blow in the wind while I pet the dogs that lay at my
feet. I get a content feeling knowing that I am saving money
today, and not needing to go anywhere. Enjoying my job does
not compare to anything money could buy me. I like that I can
create the atmosphere that I want. You can't always do that in
an office. I've always liked dogs. It's a bit weird when you think
about but my grandfather's name was Jack Russell! My advice
is to keep it small and don't get greedy. I hope that you may

find a slogan for your company that truly reflects what you believe.

I truly believe, "Your pet's happiness is my success." I wish you outstanding success with your business.